# Arthur Miller

# A PLAYWRIGHT'S LIFE AND WORKS

## ENOCH BRATER

with 70 black and white illustrations

**Thames & Hudson**

For my parents, and for my brothers

p. 1  Arthur Miller in front of the Brooklyn Bridge,
New York, 1954

opposite  Arthur Miller with the script of *Broken
Glass*, Roxbury, Connecticut, 1994

© 2005 Thames & Hudson Ltd, London

First published in 2005 in hardcover in the United States
of America by Thames & Hudson Inc., 500 Fifth Avenue,
New York, New York 10110

thamesandhudsonusa.com

Library of Congress Catalog Card Number 2005920673

ISBN-13:  978-0-500-51242-5
ISBN-10:  0-500-51242-6

Printed and bound in China by Midas Printing Ltd

# CONTENTS

Most people who have heard of Arthur Miller
know him as the author of *Death of a Salesman* and the playwright who
was once married to Marilyn Monroe. What most people don't know
about Arthur Miller is that he was also a master carpenter. For almost
fifty years he lived in an old farmhouse in Roxbury, Connecticut, which
he rebuilt mostly on his own, including the roof. When the house
burned down in 1983, destroying notebooks, memorabilia and works in
progress, he had it reconstructed along the lines of his original design.
He made most of the furniture, including the desk he wrote on, by himself; and he remained as proud of his mahogany tables as he was of anything he had ever written. All of his carpentry has the same solidity and
durability audiences all over the world have come to appreciate in his
famous work for the stage. "I never wrote a play," he said in 1986, "that
my Uncle Max couldn't understand." (Asked if Miller did indeed have
an uncle named Max, his sister, the actress Joan Copeland, demurred,
"Not in this lifetime.")

Arthur Miller, New York, 1962

Arthur Asher Miller was born in New York City on October 17, 1915. His brother Kermit, the better athlete and the better student, was three years older; and his sister Joan was born in 1922. Their parents were Augusta Barnett, a first-generation American, and Isidore Miller, an immigrant from Eastern Europe whose first home in Manhattan was on the Lower East Side, where his father ran a clothing business called S. Miller & Sons. By the time their second son arrived, Gussie and Izzy, as they were known to their relatives, had moved to the top floor of a six-story apartment house at 45 West 110 Street facing the north side of Central Park. They were well-off. The playwright's father, who was the owner of Miltex Coat and Suit Company located in the Garment District, took a chauffeured car to work. Gussie's parents lived around the corner, and in summers the extended family rented a bungalow in Rockaway Beach, the setting of Miller's short story "I Don't Need You Anymore." All three children took piano lessons. Miller went to P.S. 24 on West 111 Street, the same school his mother had attended; his best friend was Sidney Franks, who lived in the same building and whose father was a banker. Miller was in Hebrew school by the time he was "seven or eight" and had his bar mitzvah in 1928. His parents were not religious, but they observed most of the rituals that other New York Jewish families did. All four grandparents spoke Yiddish.

Isidore Miller's business was a success, at one time, according to Martin Gottfried, employing 800 workers. But like many entrepreneurs of the time, he invested heavily in the stock market. When the Crash came in 1929, he struggled for two years to keep Miltex going before giving up. He moved his family to Brooklyn, "Willy

Arthur Miller as a young boy (left), with his elder brother Kermit

Loman territory." There was still enough money to buy a house at 1350 East Third Street; in the backyard the young Miller planted a pear tree and an apple tree (the latter was felled in a storm, prefiguring the opening scene of his 1947 drama *All My Sons*). Gussie's sisters, Annie Newman and Esther Balsam, already lived on the same block. Miller was suddenly surrounded by cousins; "all I knew about," he said, "was my family." He spent long hours exploring the new neighborhood on his Columbia Racer and discovered the world he would later represent in *The American Clock*. Obsessed with sports, he went to the ice-skating rink on Ocean Parkway and played football on a vacant lot on Avenue M and Gravesend Avenue with "the Epstein twins," who later wrote "the penultimate script for *Casablanca*." They mostly argued about their games. He read Gertrude Stein and remembers being "mesmerized by Hemingway." He woke up at 4:30 in the morning and used his bicycle to deliver freshly baked bread and bagels before going off to school; when his racer was stolen, he found part-time work in an automobile supplies store. His brother, "Kerm," went on to New York University after he left James Madison High School, but Miller set his sights, unrealistically, on Stanford.

Miller's eventual enrollment at the University of Michigan was preceded by two letters of rejection. When he graduated from the new Abraham Lincoln High School on Ocean Parkway in Brooklyn in 1933, he needed four faculty members to write letters of recommendation; he could find only three. He had flunked algebra three times, and the rest of his record—both at Lincoln and at James Madison, where he spent his first two high-school years, mostly playing football (resulting in a serious leg injury that later kept him out of military service)—was similarly lackluster. Turned down in 1933, he applied again in 1934 because, as he said in October 2000, "Michigan was one of the few places that took writing seriously." Four years later he told the theater director Mark Lamos that "in those days creative writing in college was not accepted as an academic course. Harvard had a course in playwriting.

Abraham Lincoln High School on Ocean Parkway in Brooklyn, New York

They got rid of it; they were embarrassed." When Miller received his second disappointing letter of rejection from Michigan, he was emboldened to respond to the Dean of the College, telling him that he had been working hard and "had turned into a much more serious fellow." Years later, writing for *Holiday* magazine in 1953, he recalled that the Dean said he "would give me a try, but I had better make some grades. I could not conceive of a dean at Columbia or Harvard doing that." Looking back at this probationary period, Miller reflected in his eighty-fifth year, "I still can't believe Michigan let me in."

What brought Arthur Miller, a New Yorker, to a small Midwestern college town like Ann Arbor? First and foremost, tuition was cheap; and these were, after all, some of the toughest Depression years. Tuition was free, of course, at a more likely choice for someone from his background: City College, now part of the City University of New York. This had long been the intellectual center for boys and girls born to parents like Miller's, Polish Jews who worked the "schmata trade." "I tried going to City College at night," Miller said. "But I was working during the day and I kept falling asleep in class. After a few weeks, I dropped out."

Isidore Miller, businessman to the core, was amazed to hear that any school would pay students money for writing. His son told him about the Avery Hopwood Awards, built from a legacy given by a Michigan alumnus who had made a fortune on Broadway with plays like *The Best People* and such slight bedroom farces as *Getting Gertie's Garter* and *Up in Mabel's Room*. Miller's father was impressed, but reminded him that he had to make some money first—$500 for tuition fees and living expenses—before trying his hand at the Hopwoods.

For two years Miller worked at Chadwick-Delamater, a gigantic warehouse for automobile parts located on the site that in 1963 became the Lincoln Center for the Performing Arts. He earned $15 a week working for a "very dour, pasty-faced, very neat" boss named Wesley Moulton. "The area was a kind of slum," he wrote in *New York* magazine in 2000, "with a lot of saloons, working-class bars, and boarded-up houses." The company had never before hired a Jew, and at first wouldn't consider Miller when he answered their newspaper ad. But his former boss in Brooklyn intervened, telling Moulton that this young man knew "more about parts than most of you guys, so if you don't give him a job there's only one reason." At Chadwick-Delamater, Miller remembered, he "was the only Jew. The guy who worked there after me was an Italian. They hated him, too."

In the years before superhighways, and before the Pennsylvania Turnpike was completed, it took a long time to get from New York City

Students changing classes on "the Diag," the center of the University of Michigan campus, Ann Arbor, 1930s

to southeastern Michigan. "The bus had no fixed route in those days," Miller recalled. "It just took folks where they wanted to go." He hitch-hiked part of the way and was so tired when he got to Ann Arbor that he slept for two days; but once there he "felt at home. It was a little world....My friends were the sons of diemakers, farmers, ranchers, bankers, lawyers, doctors, clothing workers and unemployed relief recipients. They came from every part of the country and brought all their prejudices and special wisdoms. It was always so wonderful to get up in the morning. There was a lot learned every day." Miller remembered "going to hear Kagawa," the Japanese philosopher,

Miller while a student at the University of Michigan

and "how, suddenly, half the audience stood up and walked out because he had used the word Manchukuo," which is Japanese, for the Chinese province of Manchuria. "As I watched the Chinese students excitedly talking outside on the steps of Hill Auditorium, I felt something about the Japanese attack on China I had not felt before." As an under-graduate at one of the great publicly supported institutions of higher learning in the United States, the young Miller was attracted to what we would now call diversity in progressive, liberal education. Michigan, for example, provided a far less hostile environment to students from his background, especially as compared to Ivy League schools back East, where quotas against Jews were still being enforced. In Ann Arbor his fellow students included the future writer Norman Rosten, MIT president Jerome Wiesner and CBS television anchorman Mike Wallace.

During his first year at the University of Michigan, Miller lived in Elnora Nelson's rooming house on South Division Street. She was the widow of a dentist and made all residents store their luggage in a large wooden barrel in the attic containing old teeth (none with gold crowns, Miller discovered). His housemates included Harmon L. Remmel and Henry Carl Reigler, both from Little Rock, Arkansas; Keith and Bob Duber from just north of Ann Arbor; Paul B. Cares, a doctoral student; Charles S. Cook, who was later killed in World War II; Bob Danse; and William and Mary Tommy Lee from Kentucky, who occupied an apartment on the first floor and were great bridge players. "All of us living in the Nelson house got to play bridge with them," Remmel remembered.

That year Miller and several of his housemates took meals at a small "mom and pop" restaurant around the corner run by a family named Helper. Later, when Miller moved into an attic room on 411 North State Street, where he paid $1.75 a week, he sometimes ate at the Wolverine Eating Club located in the basement of Lane Hall. The club's cook, Anna Panzer, reported that they fed about 250 people three meals a day (she was assisted by John Ragland, who later became Ann Arbor's first African-American lawyer). About forty students, including Miller, helped with the prep and cleanup in exchange for free meals, while the rest paid $2.50 a week. At the time Miller earned $15 a week feeding past-prime vegetables to thousands of mice at 4:00 P.M. every day in Professor Frank H. Clark's laboratory, which was housed at the edge of town near the old Ann Arbor Coal Yard. In his autobiography, *Timebends*, Miller recalls trudging two miles each way.

Miller first made his mark as a writer in Ann Arbor at the *Michigan Daily*. "I remember writing a story about a professor who made the startling discovery that people were fat because they ate too much." In another article he interviewed a local official who claimed that the projects supported by the Tennessee Valley Authority were "unconstitutional"; while he was checking the galley proofs, he heard on the radio that the courts had decided otherwise. Housed in the Student Publications Building at 420 Maynard Street, the student newspaper, Miller said, "had traditionally been in the hands of fraternities, which tend to be

The Student Publications Building at 420 Maynard Street, Ann Arbor, as it looked in the 1930s

# Faculty Men Welcome Controversial Social Questions In Class Discussions

### By ARTHUR A. MILLER

Should a teacher bring into his classroom controversial social and economic questions?

Four replies to that problem inspired by the findings of a commission of educators, which reported to the congress of the National Education Association last week in St. Louis, were given yesterday by Prof. Preston W. Slosson of the history department, Prof. Lawrence Preuss of the political science department, and Prof. Arthur E. Wood of the sociology department.

The report of the commission, drawn up after four years of study, read in part: "The great need is for a school program (in the social studies) that will deal boldly and firmly with the problems of the age, neither giving way to hysteria on the one hand nor clinging blindly to tradition on the other . . . "

### Political Control A Menace

Responding to the question of the duty of teachers to foster discussion of controversial matter in class, Professor Slosson stated:

"Should a teacher deal with controversial subjects? Well, there can be no question of that. About two-thirds of all philosophy, sociology, economics, and politics, and perhaps one-third of history, and even certain advanced phases of the natural-science and philological and literary studies involve disputed theories. The only question is in what manner the teacher should approach these battle grounds.

"The most essential thing is, I think, that he should make clear that disputed matters are disputed and not give dogmatic solutions on his own authority. He should certainly state his own opinion, for if he has studied the matter he will probably have one, and why should he conceal it from his own students?

"Let me take a concrete instance from my own field — modern history.

An article by Miller in the *Michigan Daily*, March 1, 1936

## Michigan Daily

### BOARD OF EDITORS

| | |
|---|---|
| Thomas H. Kleene | *Managing Editor* |
| Thomas E. Groehn | *Associate Editor* |
| John J. Flaherty | *Associate Editor* |
| Dorothy S. Gies | William R. Reed |
| Josephine T. McLean | |

### DEPARTMENTAL BOARDS

*Publication Department*
Thomas Kleene, Chr.
Clinton B. Conger
Robert Cummins
Richard G. Hershey
Ralph W. Hurd
Fred W. Neal

*Sports Department*
William R. Reed, Chr.
George Andros
Fred Buesser
Raymond Goodman
Fred DeLano

*Reportorial Department*
Thos. Groehn, Chr.
Joseph S. Mattes
Elsie A. Pierce

*Editorial Department*
John J. Flaherty, Chr.
Arnold S. Daniels
Marshall D. Shulman

Thomas Kleene     John Flaherty
William Reed     Thomas Groehn

### REPORTERS

E. Bryce Alpern
Lester Brauser
William DeLancey
Carl Gerstacker

Arthur A. Miller
William C. Spaller
William E. Shackleton
Clayton Hepler

Richard Sidder
I. S. Silverman
Tuure Tenander
Robert Weeks

### TRYOUTS

Art Baldauf
Neil Ball
James Barco
Burton Benjamin
Philip Buchen
James Dunlap
Joe Dunlap
Robert Elliott
Mortimer Falk
Stewart Fitch
Richard Forsyth
Milton Fraskel
Brinton Freeman
Harold Garn

Joseph Gies
Earl Gilman
Horace Gilmore
Lester Goda
Roy Heath
Emmanuel Hecht
Irving Hilman
John Hilton
Paul Jones Kent
S. R. Kleiman
Richard Knowe
Sidney Kurnitsky
Howard Johnson
Herbert Ley

Nelson Lindenfeld
Irvin Lisagor
Stuart Low
Edward Magdol
Albert Mayio
Robert McAuliffe
Harlan McCain
Lawrence McKay
Allan Michelson
Robert Mitchell
Ben Moorstein
Carl Nelson
James Palms
William Parnham

Robert Perlman
Glen Phelps
Marvin Reider
Frederick Reinheimer
Leonard Rosenman
Jacob Rosengarten
William Sizemore
Eugene Snyder
Vanderbilt Spader
Fred Thomson
Jack Van Deusen
Carl Viehe
Harry Wise
Don Zimmerman

Haskell   La Marca   Silverman   Jacobs   Brauser   Hepler   Smith   Mattes   Weeks
Hershey   Sidder   Alpern   Daniels   Spaller   Tenander   Shackleton   Andros   Buesser
     DeLano   Hurd   Conger   Shulman   Weissman   Neal   

*Page 254*

Miller's name in the staff box, under "Reporters," *Michigan Daily*, May 21, 1935

conservative." But all over the country "people were going bankrupt—they were looking for another voice." When he joined the *Daily* in his sophomore year, "it was just beginning to gain attention from national wire services for its reporting on professors who were expressing political and economic views." The name "Arthur A. Miller" first appeared in the paper's staff box on May 21, 1935. In those years it was still being printed in seven-column format; Miller had his first byline three days later. Based on an Associated Press source, the headline is ripe with dramatic foreshadowing: "Anti-Red Bill Sent to Senate."

Reporting on the Dunckel-Baldwin anti-radical bill, making it a felony to advocate the overthrow of the government, the fiery cub reporter begins his coverage in Lansing, the state capital: "Before a gallery packed with more than 400 protesters…some of whom were university students, the house passed the anti-violent overthrow measure while representatives on opposing sides nearly came to blows." The bill passed 61-28, but not before demonstrators in the gallery were rebuked for disorder by the Speaker Pro-tem: "The spectators were mostly opposed to the measure, many of them wearing tags with the slogan, 'Don't pass 262', on them…Immediately before its passage, the sponsors of the measure seemed to be acceding to the negative pressure, since they offered arguments only spasmodically."

Miller's reporting for the *Michigan Daily* falls into two categories: one dealing with campus events of a nonpolitical nature, the other reflecting his attraction and growing commitment to progressive causes. His first byline for an original piece not based on another news service appears on October 11, 1935, when he writes about "Mice of Many Colors," a reflection of his part-time work in Professor Clark's laboratory. On November 9 he covers a story on the Medical School with the headline "Scientists See And Hear What Dog's Brain Cells Are Doing." Four months later there is a shift in assignments. On March 1, 1936, he reports on the National Education Association meeting in St. Louis, Missouri. The lead paragraph reads: "Should a teacher bring into his classroom controversial social and economic questions?" Two days later Miller writes about the looming 20 per cent reduction in state contributions to relief payments, unless local governments can make up the shortfall—a setback for the WPA program that was part of the Roosevelt administration's New Deal. Miller's byline appears "above the fold" for the first time on March 12, 1936 for a big story on the Michigan Student Assembly symposium on "Fascism, Naziism and Hearst."

According to his college friend and housemate Harmon Remmel, Miller spent his early years at Michigan "always involved with one cause or another." And it was at the *Daily* that he soon found it possible to reconcile his journalistic and political interests. That opportunity came in the form of a signed editorial published on October 11, 1936, when Miller responded to remarks made at the Michigan Union by the vice-chairman of the Chrysler Corporation. "Hitler is doing a great job," James C. Zeder asserted. "He's carrying on, he's getting his house in order." It was unusual for an editorial to be signed by only one member of the *Daily* staff, or to be signed at all. Miller made the most of the occasion: "In other words you mean labor in concentration camps working for whatever you choose to pay them. You mean that labor strikes and efforts of labor to make a living wage under decent conditions are 'crimes against the state'." When Zeder admitted to the president of the university that he preferred fascism over communism, Alexander G. Ruthven demurred: "We are not confronted with a choice between fascism and communism, but we cannot survive, we cannot achieve peace without the recognition of our responsibility for the welfare of others." With pointed irony, the fiery editorialist takes President Ruthven's observation one step further: "Fascism has not one iota of 'responsibility for the welfare of others.' So thanks again, Herr Zeder. But we advise if we may, that you change your opinion of the college man. HE is not a sap!" The next year Miller drove east with Ralph Neaphus, a friend determined to join the Abraham Lincoln Brigade and fight the fascists in the Spanish Civil War. Miller decided not to go with him, and returned to Ann Arbor. Months later Neaphus, aged 23, was dead.

Miller's final entry in the *Michigan Daily* appeared as a letter to the editor on May 31, 1937, when he was no longer a staff member. Writing in support of a sit-down strike by labor organizers in Washtenaw County, he objects to the right-wing position taken by "C.B.C." published the day before: "I think his logic rears up and kicks him in the face." Assuring his audience that they are all "good Americans," Miller concludes by noting that "good Americans, like good elephants, never forget tea parties, especially the Boston kind. But with one reservation under the belt. The Boston Indians never even built the tea." Asked why he gave up writing for the *Daily*, he responded that he was getting tired of sticking to "the facts"; he was quickly becoming "a lot more interested in making them up."

One of Miller's stories that did not make it into the pages of the *Michigan Daily* concerned a racist incident that took place in sports-minded Ann Arbor in 1934–35. The Wolverine football team, which included an undergraduate from Grand Rapids who later went on to become President Gerald R. Ford, was scheduled to play against Georgia Tech. The team from Atlanta refused to play on the same field with Ford's African-American teammate, Willis Ward. The official story was that Ward chose not to play after Georgia Tech protested his presence. (Michigan administrators backed down; Ward was sent off to scout another game in Wisconsin.) Miller's friends from Arkansas, Remmel and Reigler, knew one of the Tech players named Pee Wee Williams from high school, and and took Miller to meet with members of the Southern team, to protest and appeal to their sense of fair play. Not only did the visiting team rebuff "the Yankee" Miller in "salty language," but told him they would actually kill Ward if he set foot on the Michigan gridiron. Miller was furious. He "went immediately to the office of the *Michigan Daily* and wrote an article," Remmel said, "but it was not published." Years later President Ford, who graduated from the University of Michigan in 1935 and considered Miller "a lifelong friend," referred to the same incident when he spoke in support of affirmative action at the School of Public Policy named in his honor.

GARGOYLE

OCTOBER, 1937      PRICE 15c

Seven Freshman Girls
Campus Picto-Crime

Tunre Tenander
Arthur Miller

# You Simply Must Go to College

### By ARTHUR A. MILLER

*Twice Hopwood Winner, Author of "They Too Arise."*

REALLY, WE COLLEGE PEOPLE are the pick of the crop. Whatever these reformers say about education being all wet is just so much melonwater and anybody who has visited our college community will agree. Education is fitting us for life and already we are making our influence felt even before we have received our diplomas, and everybody knows that the full brunt of our influence isn't supposed to be felt until after we have our diplomas well in hand.

In short, the way we college people are going to raise the standards of conduct and thought is already apparent. It will not be long before the United Press will say, "As Ann Arbor Goes, So Goes the Nation." That's how important each and every one of us light beacons are and the best way to prove it is to examine our own well-lit community.

Everybody knows that the only first-class indication of the extent of a civilization is the home. Even Mr. Landon acutely remarked, "Everywhere I go in America I see people living together in families," so you see I'm not alone in my opinion. We must look to the home, and in this case, the Ann Arbor student's room. It will show how the light of learning has illuminated such a vast city as ours. But since we can't properly enter any house, come with me as we look for a room. That is, make believe you actually want to live in Ann Arbor as so many college people already do.

First we spy a sign saying there is a room for rent and we walk up the front steps of the house. Perhaps it will take me a few minutes to pry your leg out of the hole in the step but this is no reason for discouragement because we have plenty of time and one leg in the hole is better than two. There is, I may say without fear of contradiction, no step in Ann Arbor which has a hole big enough for two legs. As much can be said for our rooms.

We ring the doorbell and wait. Then we knock lightly on the door, and wait. Then we peek through the window, and wait. Then we softly open the door and are comforted to see our prospective landlady sitting a few feet away with her feet flat on the floor. She is relatively young, in spirit, and as she rises and approaches us she tunes her left ear with her right hand. She is very serious because she is thinking of how to make you comfortable. I say, "Have you any singles?" And she says, "Why, yes. Taxes are up and coal is up. You want to come up?" And she smiles *Mona Lisaly*. We smile also and follow her upstairs. We stop at the first landing but she turns and we follow her up another flight and we stop again and she turns and we follow again for another flight. At each floor, of course, there is a different odor to accommodate different personalities (as the psychology department advocates). Truthfully speaking, though, we college people have always made it a point to smell differently even before we are awarded our diplomas.

Now although it is broad daylight it is dark up here because, as anybody will

tell you, darkness is best for that deep concentration of which college people do so much. Our lady opens the door of the room with some difficulty (there is a bookcase with three legs leaning against it) and enters. We do the same and she stands propping up the bookcase with her left hand because her right hand is still tuning her ear with which she must listen to everything we say, in order to learn, (naturally). We look around the room and you walk toward the window but before I can give you warning, you are hanging from an electric wire by the neck but you are not shocked because all our wires are insulated, as the electrical engineering department advises. I cut you down and explain softly that it is better not to have wall plugs because you can't move them around like you can hanging wires which also make a room more interesting. That's another way education helps college peo-

ple make their lives great adventures. We have learned to chalk up every mishap to experience, which, with proper care, becomes wisdom after getting a diploma.

When you are breathing regularly again you inhale and stretch your arms out and if you are a big young man you may break the fingernails on the middle fingers of both hands against the walls because you haven't yet acquired the judgment of distances which most students get the first year in physical training classes. It aids in distinguishing a big room from a little one.

Next you lie down on the bed just to try it out and are surprised, in a small way, to find your feet so close to your face. But you are even more surprised to find that your behind is not resting on the floor, as it would in an illiterate town, and when I lift you out you see that just at the spot where it would find its place, there is a hole. The landlady says it is there to let you inform the man below when you are in bed so he can turn his radio off. With we trained men there is no guesswork permitted and the human error element is completely eliminated, except, in this case, for its most backward part which we are not sure we want to eliminate at the present stage of investigation.

The time has come for the conversation. I say, "Where is the bathroom?" For a moment she looks lost, but recovering, she says, "Downstairs. There is a light by the mirror." I glance at you with the pride of my heritage and I say, "May we see it?" She smiles and says, "Well, perhaps . . . maybe if you come back tomorrow it'll be better." I ask politely, "Why not now?" And she says, "Well you see my husband hasn't taken the coal out of the bathtub yet," and she smiles again, this time daintily. I explain to you that college people must be kept absolutely toasty in the winter and you understand.

By this time we have been inside long enough to have exhaled a bit of bad air so I try to open the window. "That's painted in tight," our lady says, and I say, "When was it painted?" But she, keeping to truth, confesses she is not old enough to remember, so right there you can see how our presence has changed human nature.

The moment has arrived. I cross my feet and lean on one and scratch my head, looking around. "What's the rent?" I ask. Now you can observe how wonderful our influence has been. Instead of saying so much a week, just like that, our lady who has lived within the perifery of our light for some years puckers up her lips, smiles wryly, hunches over a little to look even more incapacitated, and says, "Two thousand freshmen registered." We smile, thoroughly proud at her information.—a woman of her age—, and we offer, "How much did you say?" And she says, "We

*(Continued on page twenty-four)*

Not all of Miller's journalistic writings at Michigan were weighted with so much activism. He also contributed to the *Gargoyle*, the student humor magazine. Miller contributed two pieces: the first, entitled "You Simply Must Go to College," appeared in October 1937. The second appeared a few months later, in January 1938. "The Rosten" is a satirical piece about his friend Norman, a year ahead of him at Michigan. Revealing a facility for the kind of ironic edge we might associate with a mature work like *The Price*, the undergraduate writer, who now signed himself "Art Miller," characterizes his reclusive and bohemian colleague as someone who "practically lives on paper clips." They remained friends for years, up until the point Miller broke with him for "cashing in" on the notoriety of his relationship with Marilyn Monroe.

The most productive writing Miller did as an undergraduate at the University of Michigan was the three playscripts he submitted to the Hopwood Awards Committee, *No Villain*, *Honors at Dawn* and *The Great Disobedience*. Paul Mueschke, an English teacher at the university, had quickly been impressed by Miller's response to the classical Greek plays they studied in class, and also noticed his remarkable facility as a clear and concise analyzer of literary texts—a talent that seems to have eluded his high school instructors back in Brooklyn.

The first play that Miller wrote, however, was in a literature class taught by Erich Walter, who later served in the Office of the Dean. Miller asked if he could rework an assignment in dialogue form, and his instructor agreed. Walter was a stern critic—"he was capable of liking half a sentence, but not the other half"—though years later Miller still remembered how his teacher's midwestern accent did "considerable violence" to the New York rhythms he had built into his text.

Walter referred his promising student to Kenneth Rowe, a popular colleague who taught demanding courses in dramatic literature and playwriting. "Rowe, while I'm sure he wanted to teach me a lot, taught me really only one thing, and that was that I could hold the stage with dialogue. He acquainted me with the history of the theater and with the

Arthur Miller's first story in the *Gargoyle*, October 1937

development of various forms, and it was a quick way of getting educated." Rowe later published *Write That Play!*, a manual scrupulously read by students curious about learning "the mechanics of the trade." He "may not have created a playwright (no teacher ever did)," Miller said, "but he surely read what we wrote with the urgency of one who actually had the power to produce the play." Before enrolling in Professor Rowe's playwriting class, Miller said he had "wanted to be a writer" only "in a vague way": "I was trying to write stories, unsuccessfully. When I got [to Ann Arbor] I hadn't seen any plays to speak of, maybe two or three plays in my life." Rowe's students worked on such elementary principles as narrative exposition, character development, the delayed entrance of a central character, the surprise ending and the virtue of calibrating the rising action of a play. His students read a lot of Ibsen. "You may not have heard of this Norwegian playwright," Rowe was famous for telling his impressionable undergraduates, "but by the time you leave here you will know who he is." (Years later Miller prized Ibsen for being "as much a mystic as a realist.") R. W. Cowden, chair of the English Department, remembered the young Miller as "a wide awake Jewish boy and so much interested in writing that every now and then he jeopardized his scholastic standing here at Michigan in order to work on his plays. He does have talent [and] his heart is in it." Miller said on a visit to Ann Arbor in March 2004, "Writing plays seemed the best way to confront the audience, to speak about what we were feeling." Prose "seemed to be remote by comparison."

Miller wrote *No Villain* in six days during spring break in 1936. Jim Doll, the son of his landlord on North State Street, was a theater costume designer who answered many of Miller's innocent questions about the specifics of moving characters around on a stage space. Miller's only theater experience consisted of a non-speaking part he played as a freshman in a student production of Shakespeare. ("I played a bishop in *Henry VIII*. Thank God I had no lines. I had a big hat.") The storyline in *No Villain* concerns Abe Simon, a coat manufacturer like Miller's father, who is faced with financial ruin when a strike of shipping clerks prevents him from delivering his goods. ("For my family," the playwright admitted in

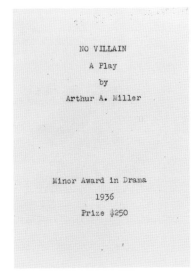

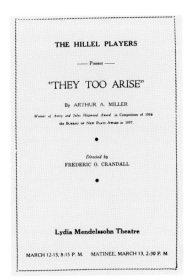

Typescript of *No Villain*, 1936

Title page from the program of
*They Too Arise*, 1937

1992, "the workers were always a big pain in the ass.") *No Villain* struggles
hard to present the question of social justice within a framework of
moral responsibility; father duels with son as each embodies the conflict
between private interest and the public good. "We've got to change the
world!" is this play's cry of embattled youth. But, as the title implies, there
are no villains. As Christopher Bigsby notes, "the characters are all victims of a system which alone is evil." When he finished the play, Miller
remembers running through the deserted streets of Ann Arbor, then back
across North University Avenue, "my head in the stars," feeling for the
first time the "magical force of making marks on a paper and reaching
into another human being, making him see what I had seen and feel my
feelings—I had made a new shadow on the earth." He submitted the
script to the Hopwood Awards Committee that same spring under the
pseudonym "Beyoum." He won $250 and the Minor Award for Drama.

"Beyoum," predicted Alfred Kreymborg, one of the national judges
for the Hopwoods in 1936, "is one of the contestants who should be
heard from." The young playwright revised his script the next year and,
giving it a new title, *They Too Arise*, entered this version in the national

Miller (seated third from left) as the Bishop of Lincoln in a student production of Shakespeare's rarely performed *King Henry VIII*, Ann Arbor, 1934–35

contest sponsored by the Theatre Guild's Bureau of New Plays. Miller won a scholarship of $1,250. (Another winner in the same competition was Thomas Lanier—later Tennessee—Williams; he was unable to take advantage of the award, dropped out of the University of Missouri and went back to work as a shoe clerk.) *They Too Arise* was produced in Ann Arbor and Detroit by the B'nai B'rith Hillel Foundation. (Frederic O. Crandall directed the play at the Lydia Mendelssohn Theatre at the Michigan League on March 12 and 13, 1937.) Miller returned to *No Villain* for a third time during the period between April 1938 and March 1939. This time the play, re-titled *The Grass Still Grows*, was a comedy, described by Kenneth Rowe as "a happy blend of serious and hilarious, sentiment and philosophical reflection." Miller's playwriting teacher was now referring to his student's plays as "the Abe Simon Trilogy."

In 1937 Miller won a second Hopwood Award for another strike play, *Honors at Dawn*. Paul Mueschke, who served as an internal judge, wrote that the manuscript submitted under the pseudonym "Corona" was "superior to the other entries" and compared "quite favorably with other full-length proletarian plays of recognized merit. *Honors at Dawn* should be carefully revised and given a campus production if possible." In this play Miller draws not only upon his familiarity with university life, but also on his experience in the automobile parts warehouse in Manhattan, material he was to explore much later in *A Memory of Two Mondays*. Working in the same vein as established playwrights like Sidney Kingsley, Elmer Rice and Clifford Odets (especially in *Waiting for Lefty*), Miller's plotline, involving union recognition in the fight for a living wage, reflects in part the narrative drive that impressed the external evaluators, Yale theater scholar Allardyce Nicoll and playwright Percival Wilde (a third judge, Susan Glaspell, was less convinced). "Corona has the ability to work out an idea interestingly, logically, and dramatically," wrote Wilde in his report to the committee. "The writing is honest, fresh, and stimulating" and "there is a definite illusion of life brought about by good character observation."

Becoming more sophisticated and assertive, and armed with two Hopwoods, Miller joined an ad-hoc Laboratory Workshop Committee, adding his name to a letter addressed to the school's Committee on Theater Practice and Policy, chaired by Professor J. A. Bursley. Dated January 21, 1938, the manifesto outlines a series of student-initiated suggestions for strengthening training in technical aspects of theater production at Michigan. At the same time, Miller's third entry to the Hopwood competition, a prison play he called *The Great Disobedience*, was not successful. Judges found it "too turgid"; it came in a disappointing second place. Originally written as an assignment for Kenneth Rowe's playwriting class, *The Great Disobedience* stems from the weekend visits Miller made to Jackson State Penitentiary, where his classmate, Sid Moscowitz, after doing well in only one course in elementary psychology, had been appointed psychologist for the entire prison. His job was to keep "six thousand inmates from going crazy." The visits elicited a strong emotional response from Miller; he returned to Ann Arbor each time determined to write a crusading social protest play about prison reform. *The Great Disobedience*, Miller said, "was the first I had ever researched; I wanted to get out of myself and use the world as my subject. And here was the system's malign pressure on human beings waiting to be exposed." Unknown to Miller, Tennessee Williams was working on *Not About Nightingales*, an intense drama about a hunger strike in a Pennsylvania high-security prison, that very same year.

Miller continued to work on *The Great Disobedience* after he left Michigan. At one point he was thinking about a streamlined version as a possibility for the Federal Theater Project, where Norman Rosten was now working. Professor Rowe urged him, however, to move in a different direction, away from the agit-prop mechanics he felt were a dead-end. Miller believed he might still be able to save the play if, as he told Rowe, he could "do it direct, clean, Greek-like." He toyed with the idea of a rewrite using "levels, lights, two choruses, and verse." The prominent acting coach Lee Strasberg looked at the script and "praised it"; there was an even chance that it might "go to [the actor] Maurice Evans." But nothing came of this idea and Miller, discouraged, reluctantly abandoned the project.

In 1938 Miller returned to New York with a strong letter of endorsement from Kenneth Rowe addressed to his connections at the Federal Theater Project. Miller was put to work writing radio plays, coauthoring one with Norman Rosten called *Listen My Children*. Designed to support theater practitioners during the Depression, and under Hallie Flanagan's visionary direction, the FTP mounted now-legendary performances all across the United States, including the premiere of T.S. Eliot's *Murder in the Cathedral*, a *Macbeth* with an African-American cast and Marc Blitzstein's musical *The Cradle Will Rock*. But the FTP's days were numbered. Conservative politicians in Washington were never really comfortable with what they saw as a left-leaning theater collective. Funds were cut off in 1940 and Miller went on relief. On August 5 of the same year, "without a dime," he married Mary Grace Slattery, a young woman from a Catholic background in Lakewood, Ohio, who had been a year behind him at Michigan. They had both been student activists. When he asked her for their first date, she suggested a movie. "He didn't have any money. I treated." By the time Miller's family heard about it, the couple were already married; his Grandpa Barnett, who always wore a yarmulke and went to Sabbath services regularly, was so distraught when his daughter told him the news that he threw a clock at her. In *Timebends* Miller transforms his grandfather's negative reaction into a rich and powerful literary motif.

Miller's sister Joan said Mary Slattery was "upright, a straight arrow," and she "got to like Mary a lot," as did their mother. The newlyweds moved into a small apartment at 62 Montague Street in Brooklyn Heights, the neighborhood they were to live in for the remainder of their married life. (Eventually they were able to buy a converted stable house at 31 Grace Court.) Soon after the wedding, Miller left on a ship headed for South America to get a fresh start on a play called *The Half-Bridge*.

Crowds at a Federal Theater Project performance, New York, 1939

Brooklyn Navy Yard, New York, 1940

His hopes were riding high, but when he returned to New York with his script no one was interested in producing it.

Mary supported them, working as both waitress and editor; eventually she became the private secretary of the head of the medical books department at Harper and Brothers. Miller worked at home, finishing another unproduced play, *The Golden Years*, about Montezuma, Cortez and the conquest of Mexico. (It was eventually presented on BBC Radio 3, but not until 1987.) Miller wrote to Professor Rowe that since June 1938 he had been struggling with "two plays, a revue, four or five radio scripts, short stories, and three postcards." "Of it all," he continued, "a 4-minute radio sketch and a half-hour radio play have been accepted and produced. Net receipts, $200 less 10% commission, plus $75 for a movie, equaling $255.00." He remembered Michigan fondly: "I can see every square foot of Ann Arbor in my head and it's prettier than this city, but I'm glad I'm not back there. Here one knows the maximum opposition and a man can confront it and learn more precisely what his place is in the world. In Ann Arbor one is a little shy of taking oneself seriously because one suspects that the whole business of collegeism is not quite bedrock secure and that it is a mock-serious game played within an outer world of deadly earnestness. There are no makeup examinations here…happily."

By 1941 Miller was working in a box factory, as a scriptwriter for the sale of U.S. war bonds and as a shipfitter's helper in the Brooklyn Navy Yard. "How those ships ever stayed afloat I'll never know. None of us had the slightest idea what we were doing." Between shifts he was developing a series of radio plays. He preferred working at night, leaving his days free for writing. Between 1941 and 1942 he completed *The Pussycat and the Expert Plumber Who Was a Man*, *William Ireland's Confession* and *The Four Freedoms*. Later his work for radio grew to include adaptations of Jane Austen's *Pride and Prejudice* and Ferenc Molnar's play, *The Guardsman* (both in 1944). None of his fellow workers, a rough-and-tumble group at the Brooklyn Navy Yard, could believe he was a playwright, and Miller mostly (but not always) kept this information to himself. He was also writing poetry: "I needed it for my plays. Poetry requires a deep feeling for speech rhythm," he told Kenneth Rowe in another letter. "The only other time in my life when I felt like this is when I mastered geometry." (Years later he told Russell Baker, after the BBC adaptation of *Broken Glass* was shown in America on PBS, that he was still doing rough drafts of his dialogue in verse, for the sake of economy and concision.)

Miller also tried to write a novel. His proposal for a story billed as an "investigation to discover what exact part a man played in his own fate" earned him a small advance from the Atlantic Monthly Press. But he found himself unable to complete the book; when he finished only half of *The Man Who Had All the Luck* the publisher turned it down. (He returned to the core idea of the novel for his 1944 play of the same name.)

Late in 1943 his agent Paul Streger found him a well-paid job that allowed him to quit the nightshift at the Brooklyn Navy Yard; he received $750 a week for working on *The Story of G.I. Joe*, a Hollywood screenplay based on news reports written by the popular war correspondent Ernie Pyle. By the time the movie starring Robert Mitchum and Burgess Meredith was released, however, Miller was long gone from the project and he received no credit. Having immersed himself in military lore for the film, Miller drew upon it to complete a nonfiction book about soldiers returning from the field and the problems they encountered adjusting to civilian life. Frank E. Taylor, the editor for whom Mary was now working, published *Situation Normal* in 1944 after she called her husband's manuscript to his attention. The book was dedicated to "Lieutenant Kermit Miller, United States Infantry."

Miller wrote *All My Sons* in 1947 in a last-ditch effort to make his mark as a professional New York playwright. Three years earlier, despite winning the Theatre Guild National Award, the Broadway production of *The Man Who Had All the Luck*, had closed after only four performances. (In 1990 an updated version was successfully staged by Paul

Film still from *The Story of G.I. Joe*, 1945, with Burgess Meredith (far right)

Unwin in a joint production for the Bristol Old Vic and the Young Vic in London; and in 2002 Scott Ellis mounted a New York production for the Roundabout Theatre, featuring Chris O'Donnell.) In the interval between *The Man Who Had All the Luck* and *All My Sons*, Miller published *Focus* (1945), a formulaic but curiously compelling story about anti-Semitism in postwar America originally called *Some Shall Not Sleep*. The novel appeared the same year as Laura Z. Hobson's *Gentleman's Agreement*, which Elia Kazan adapted in 1947 for his film

Karl Swenson as David Beeves, Eugenia Rawls as Hester Falk and Dudley Sadler as Amos Beeves, in the 1944 production of *The Man Who Had All the Luck* at the Forrest Theatre in New York

with Gregory Peck, Celeste Holm and John Garfield. (*Focus* did not make it to the screen until 2001, when Neal Slavin directed William H. Macy and Laura Dern in a screenplay by Kendrew Lascelles.) Relying on a metaphor in which failing eyesight and awakening insight "focus" on ethnic tensions in workaday Manhattan and dormitory-community Queens, Miller's first novel displays the lethal consequences of race-baiting and prejudice in a society which publicly thinks a whole lot better of itself. But it was *All My Sons*, the drama of war-profiteering set

A scene from Elia Kazan's original production of *All My Sons*, Coronet Theatre, New York, 1947, with Arthur Kennedy (far right) as Chris Keller in the backyard of middle America, that was to establish Miller as a major new voice for the stage. The play was an instant sensation. With Karl Malden, Arthur Kennedy and Ed Begley in the original cast, it won the New York Drama Critics' Circle Award, even though Eugene O'Neill's new play, *The Iceman Cometh*, was running in another theater down the same block on West 47th Street. Miller celebrated the event by buying himself a Studebaker convertible.

Stella Adler, the actress and well-known teacher, once told her students that the great theme of *All My Sons* was "business vs. civilization." Miller said he was moved to write "an absolutely realistic play" when he read a newspaper account of a case in which the Wright Aeronautics Corporation of Ohio placed "Passed" tags on defective plane engines after bribing corrupt army inspectors. "The truth," Miller said, "was blinding." Employing such melodramatic devices as the long-delayed revelation of the contents of a letter written years before by a character now dead, as well as a gun that goes off in the last act, the play is nonetheless remarkable for its clarity of exposition and the ability to sustain dramatic tension and suspense. The story is a simple one, but it carries enormous moral weight. During the war Joe Keller, small-parts manufacturer, continued to sell defective components to the U.S. military after the process he patented suddenly produced hairline fractures in the mold. "You got a crack, you're out of business," he remarks. "A man can't be a Jesus Christ in this world!" Rather than take responsibility for his actions, Joe feigned illness the day the imperfections were discovered and allowed his partner, still serving a jail sentence, to take the rap. Miller's stage is emblematic but also economical: Joe's business partner was also his next-door neighbor. As the play begins, it is the convict's daughter Ann, formerly engaged to Joe's lost son Larry, who has the catalyst part. Armed with the letter, which she will use if she has to, the proverbial "girl next door" returns home from the big city to claim a new life for herself with the second son, Chris. As in Ibsen, with his "insistence on causation," the characters have already made their pact with an uneasy past; the major events have already taken place before the curtain rises. What we watch with alarming intensity is the relentless unfolding of the consequences of the choices the characters have already made. Political history, public as well as private, determines the drama we witness in the present. "I know you're no worse than most men," the surviving son says to his father, "but I thought you were better."

"I wanted to bring the life of the streets into the theater," the playwright noted, "so you could tell it to a man on a train and he would get it." Set "in the late 1940s," in pre-suburban and pre-luxurious America, where there are no fences, the play appeared at the very moment when the country, victorious in war after defeating fascism in Europe and imperialism in Japan, was "feeling good about itself." The play refused to let its audience forget the ugly side of recent events it seemed all too willing "to sweep under the rug." Despite the play's critical acclaim, the reaction to *All My Sons*, Miller remembers, "was mostly ferocious." (According to Miller's FBI file, *All My Sons* was "party-line propaganda.") In his introduction to the *Collected Plays*, published in 1957, Miller wrote that "the spectacle of human sacrifice in contrast with aggrandizement is a sharp and heartbreaking one." During World War II "war-profiteering wasn't supposed to be going on," Miller said. "Everyone knew it was going on, but it wasn't supposed to be happening." In *All My Sons*, however, to use one of the playwright's favorite phrases, "the chickens come home to roost." What Keller doesn't know, but what both he and the audience will discover in the play's heartrending conclusion, is that Larry flew off and crashed his own plane when he recognized his father's culpability after learning about the legal case involving "business" back home. Keller will kill himself, too, but not before a stunning moment of self-awareness. What Larry wanted him to know is what he finally comes to understand and embrace: that all those doomed young pilots flying planes with defective parts in Southeast Asia were, in fact, "all my sons." His exit line is both brutal and cauterizing: "And I guess they were. I guess they were." Moments later a gunshot is heard offstage.

In this play of moral choice and purposeful communal identity, the familial relationship that most concerns Miller is the increasingly volatile bond uniting Keller and his younger son, the highly idealistic but emotionally confused Chris. This family has been living a lie. Chris will be called upon to unravel the truth; in the process he will set himself free. As always in Miller, maturity comes at a price: Chris's life is purchased by a suicide. "Live! Live!" his mother Kate intones in the play's curtain line, releasing, at long last, her own pent-up emotions. Having thought that he was sending his father to the expiation of a long-overdue prison sentence, Chris is shocked as the curtain slowly falls to discover that he has condemned him, instead, to violent death.

Miller's development as a playwright in the three years separating *All My Sons* from *The Man Who Had All the Luck* is remarkable. The earlier play, which he based in part on a story told to him by Mary's mother, is in reality "a fable," a reverse Job tale. The playwright described it as "an argument with God," "a kind of fairy tale about the mystery of fate and destiny." Everything goes right for David Beeves, Miller's unprepossessing golden boy, though there is neither rhyme nor reason to explain his success. Chance similarly accounts for another character's failure: Amos, David's unlucky brother, the more likely all-American, never achieves his dream of becoming a major-league baseball star. Hard work hardly matters, nor does commitment (though a fatal flaw in their father's underground baseball diamond means that this aspiring pitcher will never realize his full potential to soar). "You die and they wipe your name right off the mailbox." The play, however, turns surprisingly inward with David's sense of impending doom. When will the gods exact a price for his charmed life? Here the crisis is psychological, though its consequences are blunted by David's continuing good fortune as the man who indeed has all the luck. In this enterprise, unnamed forces, what Thomas Hardy called "crass causality," determine every protagonist's fate.

In writing *All My Sons*, Miller moved from a formula in which figures are acted upon to the far more searching dramatic strategy in which characters are made responsible for their actions. The result is an entirely different sort of play, one that was to have enormous repercussions as Miller's career developed and expanded. Following the conventions of the family play—and Miller would be quick to point out that *King Lear* and *Oedipus Rex* are also, among other things, family plays—*All My Sons*, originally called *The Sign of the Archer*, uses the recognizable domestic framework to study its much wider implications for what the playwright called "the family of man." Within such well-established contours Miller typically centers his energy on a convincing father-son conflict, though in *All My Sons* this is by no means the only drama to command our attention. Unlike *The Man Who Had All the Luck*, where the single significant female figure, Hester Falk, is the sympathetic love-interest who becomes the loyal Mrs. David Beeves, this play features two strong roles for female actors, Kate Keller and the determined Ann Deever.

In *All My Sons* the younger woman refuses to play the secondary part. She knows that Larry will never return, and that her own homecoming will be welcomed, if at all, quite differently. Her trip from New York back to the heartland presents her with several challenges: Kate, who keeps Larry's freshly pressed suits waiting for him in his bedroom closet, is frozen by both time and delusion, while Chris, the would-be lover who has invited Ann home, is similarly frozen, overwhelmed by guilt and unable to respond physically to the woman who will always be his brother's girl. She must also cut herself off from her own brother, George, the innocent young man who enters the set as a firebrand at once inspired and trapped by the injustice done to their father. Ann therefore has her work cut out for her as she takes unfinished business into her own hands and pushes the drama forward towards its inevitable conclusion.

Kate plays a more subtle part in this tragedy, but her role is much richer, especially as revealed in a series of powerful interpretations: Rosemary Harris in Michael Blakemore's 1981 London production, Michael Learned in Jack O'Brien's as broadcast in the 1990s on PBS television and Julie Walters as directed by Howard Davies in 2000 at the

Julie Walters as Kate Keller and Catherine McCormack as Ann Deever in the 2000 production
of *All My Sons* at the National Theatre in London

National Theatre. What Kate knows when and, more importantly, what
she *allows* herself to know when, may very well be the key that unlocks
the deceit and self-deception that lie at the heart of the play. For if Kate
admits to herself the reality of her husband's cover-up, she must also
accept what she finds impossible to believe: that her son Larry is dead
and that Joe killed him. Her delayed entrance in the first scene, as Chris
and Joe discuss her likely reactions to the storm that has raged the night
before, makes her a figure of considerable intrigue. And her long monologue, the first of several she has in this work, allows her to command
the stage almost as soon as she appears. What she laments most, at least
verbally, is the loss of the tree planted as a sign of hope for the son who
has not yet returned from war, even though three years have passed.
Miller's deft symbolism cuts to the quick: the trunk felled by lightning

Film still of Burt Lancaster (second from left) and
Edward G. Robinson (second from right) in *All My Sons*, 1948

in this garden is, as might be expected, an apple tree. No wonder Mordecai Gorelik, the stage designer for the 1947 premiere, originally wanted to include a "funeral mound" on his set. This was, after all, "a graveyard play." The popular Hollywood movie, however, starring a haunted Edward G. Robinson and a virile Burt Lancaster in the principal father-son roles, set the crucial scene of their domestic confrontation indoors, on a staircase no less, highlighting what may well be the work's major weakness, its conflation of high-mindedness and melodrama.

Miller's task in *All My Sons* was formidable: how to construct a play that was on the one hand anecdotal and particular, and on the other widely and richly representative, symbolic, at times even mythic in scope, all the while observing the strict and unforgiving rules of fourth-wall realism. The demands of dramatic structure would prove even more daunting in Miller's next play, *Death of a Salesman*.

In 1949 Miller took the train from Penn Station in New York to Philadelphia for the tryout of a strange new play he had originally thought of calling *The Inside of His Head*. From early on, the work seemed to demand a stage solution as difficult as it was elusive: how to render the past, the present and the protagonist's increasingly desperate imagination as one continuous whole, without resorting to "flashbacks" (a term the playwright disliked) or the clumsy apparatus of frequent and intrusive scene breaks. The drama would be realistic, of course, but it presupposed a realism with a difference. The naturalistic sets Miller imagined for *All My Sons* and *The Man Who Had All the Luck* would not do the trick here. To make this play work, stage space would have to be explored differently by Miller, the director Elia Kazan and the brilliant and innovative designer Jo Mielziner. This much-celebrated collaboration resulted in the invention of a highly atmospheric platform set that gave *Salesman* the look and flexibility its narrative energy required. On a multi-level constructivist set, time past and time present could be in dialogue with each other as a rhythmic pattern of negotia-tion and renewal emerged. All that was needed to signal transition was stage lighting, accompanied by the haunting sound of a flute playing some-where in the distance. Given such a highly unusu-al design concept, Miller's "dream rising out of reality" might well stand the chance of finding a place for itself on the modern stage.

No one involved in the original production of *Death of a Salesman*, least of all the playwright, was sure that the gamble would work. The producer Kermit Bloomgarden, one of the play's principal backers, recommended a different title for the play. Convinced that no one would buy a ticket to a show with "death" advertised on the marquee, he suggested *Free and Clear*, highlighting Linda's monologue in the Requiem, which brings closure

Elia Kazan and Arthur Miller on the set for the Broadway production of *Death of a Salesman*, 1949

to the play. "The work I wrote is called *Death of a Salesman*," the play-wright is reported to have said. When the curtain came down on the first performance at the Locust Theatre in Philadelphia, followed by too many moments of awkward silence, the tension, as Miller relates in his autobiography, was palpable and real. A lot was at stake, not only for Miller, but "for the future of the American theater." There was, finally, thunderous applause, followed by the oddest thing of all: "men and women wept openly" and, after the applause died down, "members of the audience refused to leave and started talking to complete strangers about how deeply they had been affected by the play." Miller, who thought he had written a tough, hard-hitting exposé of the dangerous and deceptive myth of "making it in America," was entirely unprepared for the emotional punch *Salesman* delivered in performance. His play had all at once found a life of its own.

When Willy Loman, suitcase in hand, slowly walks onto the set of *Death of a Salesman* in one of the most famous stage entrances in theater

Jo Mielziner's set design for the 1949 premiere of *Death of a Salesman*

history, he begins the long requiem that finally declares itself as such in the closing moments of the play. The work, Miller said, "is written from the sidewalk instead of from a skyscraper." Unlike Willy's sons, the audience hardly needs to wait for Linda's pronouncement to understand that "the man is exhausted. A small man can be just as tired as a great man." Miller's proletarian spirit permeates the entire play: Willy Loman, the salesman working on commissions that never come, is down on his luck (not that he ever really had any); Happy, who talks big, is the perpetual assistant to an assistant; Biff, who (unlike his father) knows he's "a dime a dozen," is the ageing, fair-haired boy long gone to seed; while Linda, the homebody ignored by time, is unable to stem the tide of tragedy that soon engulfs them all, try as she might. The whole question of "Tragedy and the Common Man" that initially greeted the play, and about which the playwright has perhaps said too much, now seems rather quaint and beside the point in terms of the work's immediacy, accessibility and inter-generational appeal. Linda was right about one thing: "Attention, attention must finally be paid to such a man."

Lee J. Cobb left such an indelible impression as the first Willy Loman that it became, as with Marlon Brando's Stanley Kowalski in Tennessee Williams's *A Streetcar Named Desire*, almost impossible to separate the actor from the role. A big, burly man who could look as crumpled on stage as off, he was nonetheless a player with huge and unexpected resources of dignity and understated eloquence, all of which he brought to the part. His behavior during rehearsals was erratic (and that is putting it mildly); even a sympathetic colleague like Mildred Dunnock, the original Linda, wondered if he would be able to rise to the occasion of an opening night. That he did so with so much grace and aplomb led him to craft one of the legendary stage performances of his time.

Although we generally think of Miller as a playwright with a narrative rather than a visual imagination, *Death of a Salesman* relies on a strong sense of stage imagery: the set is Miller's play. Dwarfed beneath

Lee J. Cobb (seated left) as Willy Loman in the 1949 production of *Death of a Salesman*

looming apartment blocks that rob the sunlight from Willy's garden, the Loman house belongs to some other moment in time and a very different sense of place. This is still Brooklyn, but a reimagined Brooklyn in which windows, like dozens of threatening eyes, stare down on a diminished world and make it seem even more local and inconsequential. "There's more people now!" Willy cries out in an anger that is really despair. Most productions of *Salesman* rely on projected scenery to foreground Willy's increasing claustrophobia, yet from a scenic point of view his psychological state is rendered as something palpable, material and frighteningly real. Music, too, tells the story. Each of Willy's journeys into the past, including one double journey, is signaled by the sound of a single, plaintive flute. His father, significantly, made his own flutes by hand, then sold them himself; Willy's sample case, by contrast, contains factory-made "dry goods." Other sounds will be similarly evocative: the recorded voice of a child on tape drowns out Willy's plea for help, and Biff is cautioned against whistling in elevators (he does so anyway; the Lomans are great whistlers). Finally, when Willy's life comes crashing down all around him, we hear the cacophonous sounds of metal twisting, brakes screeching and glass shattering, followed by an ominous stage silence.

In *Salesman*, of course, as elsewhere in Miller, the play's atmospheric dimension is there to enhance the work's narrative authority and appeal. This is first and foremost the theater's most compelling tale of the dark underside of the American Dream, half-fantasy, half-phantasmagoria, essentially configured as a triumphalist and everywhere disturbing guy-culture. Willy, as we hear in the play's Requiem, was a man who "never knew who he was"; but he was also, as Miller later said, a man who "chased everything that rusts." He had all "the wrong dreams." Caught up, like most of his country, in the vain and unobtainable lure of success, which he equates with material wealth, popularity and the making of a good impression ("be well liked and you shall never want"), he realizes all too late that what he has been searching for all his life he has had all along: Biff's unqualified love. What makes the play a tragedy—and it is certainly that—is that the father's unfulfilled ambitions, rather than any insurance payouts, are the only inheritance he can offer his sons. His legacy is their peril. "I'm not bringing home any more prizes." What Biff is saying is that you will have to love me anyway. But by then it is too late. Willy drives off and kills himself.

The effect of *Salesman* on Miller's audience can be so daunting, the emotion it excites so raw, that the drama quickly becomes, despite its author's stated intentions, something quite different from a thesis play. And this may have little to do with the protagonist's socio-economic situation as a "low-man." The playwright took the name from Fritz Lang's *The Testament of Dr. Mabuse*, the 1933 film in which a detective hopes to redeem himself by exposing a gang of forgers. Duped by them instead, he shouts into a telephone to his former boss, "Lohmann? Help me, for God's sake! Lohmann!" Later in the same film, we meet the crazed detective in an asylum as he shouts into an invisible phone, "Lohmann? Lohmann? Lohmann?" "What the name really meant to me," Miller said, "was a terrified man calling into the void for help that will never come."

In performance, as recent revivals have shown, the play is a great deal more moving than the sum of its short, individual scenes. The writer discovered this himself when he brought the work to China. As part of the cultural exchange accompanying the normalization of diplomatic relations between the Chinese People's Republic and the United States during the Nixon administration, Miller was invited to supervise a major production in Beijing. He wasn't at all sure that a highly personal story about the cost of a defeated life in capitalist America would make any sense in a collectivist, communist society. But as *Salesman in Beijing*, the book he did with Inge Morath, clearly illustrates, Willy Loman's story was experienced in China as a family tragedy created in its own national image. "Remember [the character's] size," his "ugliness," Miller wrote in the notebook he kept while working on the first draft for this play. "Remember his attitude." "Remember," above all, "*pity.*"

Arthur Miller with Zhu Lin as Linda, Ying Ruocheng (the play's translator) as Willy Loman, Zhong Jiyao as Uncle Ben, Mi Tiezeng as Biff and Li Shilong as Happy in the 1983 Beijing People's Art Theatre production of *Death of a Salesman*

*Death of a Salesman* was a huge critical and box-office success when it opened in New York at the Morosco Theatre on February 10, 1949. Arthur Kennedy was featured in the role of Biff and Cameron Mitchell played Happy. The play won a Pulitzer Prize, a Tony Award and, coming just two years after *All My Sons*, Miller's second award from the New York Drama Critics' Circle. The playwright was only thirty-five years old.

In July of the same year, Kazan directed *Salesman* in London with Paul Muni as Willy Loman. A film version was released in 1952 with a mixed New York-London cast; directed by Laszlo Benedek, it featured Fredric March as Willy, Mildred Dunnock as Linda, Kevin McCarthy as

Biff and Cameron Mitchell as Happy. Fredric March had been Lee
J. Cobb's replacement in the original New York production, and later
took the show on tour.

The real test for any modern classic, however, is its ability to re-
create itself for new audiences in different times. This has certainly
held true for Miller's signature play. In 1979 Michael Rudman, then a
young director at the National Theatre in London, mounted a forceful
production in the Lyttleton Theatre, casting the veteran actor Warren
Mitchell in the role of Willy Loman. The director very much wanted to
bring the work back to Miller's roots. The playwright had been clear
about not giving the Lomans any specific ethnic identity; his aim was to
tell a story not about *some* Americans but about *all* Americans. Besides,
the drama of working-class Jewish America had already been portrayed
with clarity and vigor by Clifford Odets, whose Depression-era *Awake
and Sing!* was the single most important play presented in New York by
the Group Theatre in the 1930s. Rudman's set included minor details—
a Hebrew/English calendar, for example—in an attempt to make a
point, and Warren Mitchell used East End inflections to give his
character the authenticity his director wanted.

Among those who saw the National Theatre production was the
American film actor Dustin Hoffman. He remembered how much he
had been impressed with Lee J. Cobb in the taped version of *Salesman*
prepared for American television in the early 1950s. Hoffman brought
*Salesman* back to New York, then back to London again, casting himself
in the role of Willy Loman. With a new director in tow, Volker
Schlondorff (celebrated for his film adaptation of Günter Grass's *The
Tin Drum*), Hoffman later co-produced *Death of a Salesman* as a major
television film for CBS (though it was released in movie houses when
shown abroad). Despite a strong cast—John Malkovich in the role of
Biff, Charles Durning as the Lomans' neighbor Charley and the
Canadian actress Kate Reid in an exceptionally fine and nuanced
portrayal of Linda—film editing never succeeded in capturing the
spontaneity of the stage play's temporal fluidity. This was, however, very

John Malkovich as Biff, Kate Reid as Linda, Dustin Hoffman as Willy Loman and
Stephen Lang as Happy in the 1984 television production of *Death of a Salesman*

much Dustin Hoffman's show: even the dialogue received fine-tuning
to accommodate the actor's physical stature. (In this production Willy
became a "short" man, not a "fat" one.) Hoffman said he had been waiting all his life to play a part like this; when he began his career as a
young actor, ads for "leading man" never meant "short" and "ethnic."
His Willy Loman, like Warren Mitchell's, could be both. The telecast was
seen by an audience of twenty-five million people.

The Chicago-based director Robert Falls prepared a fiftieth
anniversary production of *Death of a Salesman* for the Goodman Theatre
as early as 1997, this time substituting a stage-revolve for the original's
platform set. Starring Brian Dennehy, who earned one of this show's
several Tony Awards when the play settled in for a sold-out run two

Kevin Anderson, Brian Dennehy and Ted Koch in the 1997 production of *Death of a Salesman* at the Goodman Theatre in Chicago

years later at the Eugene O'Neill Theatre on Broadway, *Salesman* quickly reasserted itself for a new generation of theatergoers. Falls's well-cast production, including Elizabeth Franz as Linda, clearly demonstrated that Miller's stage life was still very much in the present tense. A mere half-century after its first appearance in Philadelphia, *Salesman*, like Beckett's *Waiting for Godot*, had become an international theater icon.

Miller's initial response to the Communist witch-hunts that began in the early 1950s was an adaptation of Ibsen's *An Enemy of the People*, which he wrote for his friends, the actors Florence Eldredge and Fredric March. The play was produced in New York in 1950. "I have made no secret of my early love for Ibsen's work," Miller wrote in the *Index of*

*Censorship* in 1989, a year after his adaptation had been revived in a new production by the Young Vic in London that emphasized the play's powerful depiction of social corruption and greed in light of looming ecological disaster. In 1990 he told Jack O'Brien, who directed the show for "American Playhouse" on PBS, that he found Ibsen's 1882 hero, Dr. Stockmann, "a kind of holy fool." Yet Ibsen's theme, Miller reflected, really "concerns the crushing of the dissenting spirit by the majority, and the right and obligation of such a spirit to exist at all." The play tells the story of an idealistic doctor who discovers that the spring waters from which his spa town draws its wealth are dangerously contaminated. As Stockmann's fellow citizens realize the financial implications of his research, he comes under increasing pressure to keep silent. Miller was particularly struck by one of Dr. Stockmann's lines, which he renders as "The majority is never right until it does right." He later admitted that "this particular subject can get me very angry."

And it certainly did so at the time he was occupied in transforming Ibsen's five-act structure into three. "Those who warp the truth," he wrote in the preface to his adaptation, "must inevitably be warped and corrupted themselves." Shifting the locale from Norway to Clearwater Springs in Riverton, Maine in 1893, Miller not only Americanized the language of the play, but also its political metaphor: "I am sure that few in the first New York audience in the early '50s were terribly convinced by the play's warnings of danger to the environment. The anti-Communist gale was blowing hard and it was [that] metaphor that stood in the foreground," not "the poisoning of the public water supply by mendacious and greedy interests."

But it is *The Crucible*, Miller's most often produced play, that most significantly captures the climate of fear and the abuse of civil liberties set in motion by Senator Joseph McCarthy and other right-wing opportunists in the United States Congress. "I don't think I can adequately communicate the sheer density of the atmosphere of the time," Miller observed. "For the outrageous had so suddenly become the accepted norm." He told Christopher Bigsby that "it was really a

Fredric March (center) as Dr. Thomas Stockmann and Florence Eldredge (second from right) as Mrs. Stockmann in the 1950 Broadway production of *An Enemy of the People,* adapted from Ibsen's play by Miller

tremendous outburst of primitive human terror." In 1953 *The Crucible* opened on Broadway at the Martin Beck Theatre and won both the Tony and the Donaldson Awards; the large cast included Arthur Kennedy, Jennie Egan, George Mitchell, Cloris Leachman, Barbara Stanton, Beatrice Straight, E.G. Marshall, Madeleine Sherwood, Walter Hampden and Fred Stewart. Although Miller would not be summoned before the House Committee on Un-American Activities (HUAC) for another three years, the play already displayed his disgust with Red-baiting, his contempt for those who named names and, above all, his clear-sightedness concerning the show-trial nature of the entire enterprise.

The progressive theater community in New York quickly became an early target for McCarthy and his henchmen. Liberal, urbane and Left-leaning, many of them members of the original Group Theatre with immigrant and often Eastern European Jewish roots (like Miller himself), the entertainment industry on both coasts provided some of

Scene from the 1953 Broadway premiere of *The Crucible*

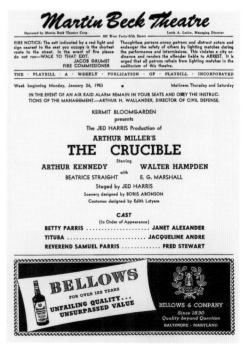

Playbill from the original New York production

the prime material HUAC needed to present its case before a provincial, puritanical and conservative America. Several members of the Group Theatre, for example, had indeed been members of the Communist Party in the 1930s, and all identified with the fight against poverty, inequality and fascism. Fifteen years later, in the first years of the Cold War, McCarthy knew "the heartland" well and how easily, especially in the dawning age of television, his Midwestern constituency as well as the truth could be manipulated. Those same live broadcasts of committee hearings would eventually prove his undoing, but in 1953 the stage was still his, as was a blacklist that stunted and in some cases ruined the careers of John Garfield, Phoebe Brand, Sam Wanamaker, Morris Carnovsky, Zero Mostel and Lee Grant. Others named names: Clifford Odets, Elia Kazan and, with a young family to feed and no visible means of support, the original Willy Loman himself, Lee J. Cobb. This was indeed, as Lillian Hellman called it, a "scoundrel time." Summoned to testify before the same committee about herself and her well-known relationship with Dashiell Hammett, she famously stood up and walked out of the chamber hearings, but not before announcing, theatrically, that she refused to cater her morality to "today's fashion." Miller's reaction to this lethal phase of McCarthyism was more muted, though it resulted in a major work for the American theater whose resonance would prove far more enduring.

In writing *The Crucible* Miller tried hard to avoid the strong emotional undertow that had an uncanny way of overwhelming the argumentative texture of works like *All My Sons* and especially *Death of a Salesman*. (Later he would admit that an audience must be made "to feel before it can be made to think.") Rather than situate the play in the contentious political climate of the McCarthyite present, he made the firm decision to look to the past not only for historical precedent but also for a controlling metaphor. "Gradually, over weeks," he wrote in *Timebends*, "a living connection between myself and Salem, and between Salem and Washington, was made in my mind—for whatever else they might be, I saw that the House Un-American Activities Committee

Senator Joseph McCarthy (foreground) swearing in Dashiell Hammett at a Senate Permanent Investigating Committee hearing on Communism, January 1953

hearings in Washington were profoundly and even avowedly ritualistic." Miller drove to the Atlantic coast of eastern Massachusetts to research letters, diaries and court records relating to the Salem witch trials of 1692, a murky period in New England history that resulted in the detention of more than 200 people. What he discovered was that nineteen of them (along with two dogs) were hanged, one was stoned to death and three died in prison after being accused of being in league with the Devil. Salem's seventeenth-century victims refused to recant their confederacy with the forces of darkness; that was their crime and their undoing. What their judges required, as in the HUAC interrogations, was a "public confession," after which they could be "let loose to rejoin the society of extremely decent people." The Salem documents told the story the playwright had been looking for: "In effect, it came down to a government decree of *moral* guilt that could be easily made to disappear by ritual speech: intoning names of fellow sinners and recanting former beliefs."

At first Miller rejected the idea of a play on this subject. "My own rationality was too strong, I thought, to really allow me to capture this wildly irrational outbreak." But before long the playwright began to shape his raw materials into a tight, four-act structure. He invented a new language for the play, one that has sometimes been disparaged as "clotted Puritanese." Yet, as the actor E.G. Marshall pointed out in a letter to the *New York Times* in 1991, the spoken dialogue in *The Crucible* was "coherent, consistent, and sometimes thrilling," and it was "certainly flavored with English speech." Miller based the stage language his characters spoke on the written documents he uncovered. For dramatic economy he fused the identity of several historical figures, though in general his research was accurate. His principal change was to raise the age of John Proctor's accuser, Abigail Williams, from 11 to 17, to account for their adultery, the sexual liaison that becomes increasingly intertwined with her false accusations

The Wonders of the Invisible World.

# OBSERVATIONS

As well *Historical* as *Theological*, upon the NATURE, the NUMBER, and the OPERATIONS of the

# DEVILS.

Accompany'd with,

I. Some Accounts of the Grievous Molestations, by DÆMONS and WITCHCRAFTS, which have lately annoy'd the Countrey; and the Trials of some eminent *Malefactors* Executed upon occasion thereof: with several Remarkable *Curiosities* therein occurring.

II. Some Counsils, Directing a due Improvement of the terrible things, lately done, by the Unusual & Amazing Range of EVIL SPIRITS, in Our Neighbourhood: & the methods to prevent the *Wrongs* which those *Evil Angels* may intend against all sorts of people among us, especially in Accusations of the Innocent.

III. Some Conjectures upon the great EVENTS, likely to befall, the WORLD in General, and NEW ENGLAND in Particular; as also upon the Advances of the TIME, when we shall see BETTER DAYES.

IV. A short Narrative of a late Outrage committed by a knot of WITCHES in *Swedeland*, very much Resembling, and so far Explaining, *That* under which our parts of *America* have laboured!

V. THE DEVIL DISCOVERED: In a Brief Discourse upon those TEMPTATIONS, which are the more Ordinary *Devices* of the Wicked One.

By Cotton Mather.

*Boston* Printed by *Benj. Harris* for *Sam. Phillips.* 1693.

Page from one of Cotton Mather's witch-hunt pamphlets, Boston, 1693

Miller standing in the cemetery at Salem, Massachusetts, where the bodies of those involved in the events he depicted in *The Crucible* are buried

of witchcraft against his wife Elizabeth. In 1996 Miller said he did not remember concentrating on the centrality of sexuality when he was working on the play: "I wasn't thinking in those terms, but that's an important element. The politically illicit always contains a germ of the sexually illicit." For Miller the play was about power "and the lust for it." He noticed, however, that almost every testimony he read in Salem "revealed the sexual theme"; the relief that came to those who testified "was orgasmic." The court even encouraged them to talk openly "about their sharing a bed with someone they weren't married to, a live human being now manacled before them courtesy of God's lieutenants." Guilt, the "guilt of illicit sexuality," had to be part of the public display. Only then could the sinner be returned to the fold. Repudiating suppressed feelings of hostility and alienation toward "standard daylight society as defined by its most orthodox proponents" would recertify and reinvigorate a threatened system of oppression—and those who held undisputed authority over it. That is why John Proctor becomes in the course of the play Miller's reluctant martyr. His refusal to tarnish his name, even in the face of certain death, is an ultimate and eloquent act of political dissent. "The longer I worked [on *The Crucible*]," Miller wrote, "the more certain I felt that as improbable as it might seem, there were moments when an individual conscience was all that could keep a world from falling."

On his way to investigate the Salem witch trials, Miller stopped off in Connecticut to see Elia Kazan and his first wife, the playwright Molly Day Thacher. It was a fateful meeting for both men, and would mark the beginning of a deep chasm in their friendship and in their professional relationship. Kazan, whose directing credits included the world premieres of several major works by Tennessee Williams, most notably *A Streetcar Named Desire*, had been summoned to appear before the House Committee on Un-American Activities, where he was later to implicate others. From their discussions, which in many ways inform the dramatic conflict in *The Crucible* as well as the core argument in the opening act of *After the Fall*, it soon became clear that Kazan was, at best, equivocating. On the one hand, to be an informer was unpalatable; on the other hand, as Kazan put it at the time, "Secrecy serves the Communists." Miller was horrified. (The two would not work together again for more than a decade.) Kazan, who had briefly been a member of the Communist Party in the 1930s, initially refused to testify when subpoenaed by HUAC. But in an executive session without publicity he changed his mind; he named a dozen people with a "pink past" he had known long ago, and on whom the committee already had testimony. In his autobiography, *Elia Kazan: A Life*, the director said that by the 1950s, after Stalin's persecutions, he had lost all respect for Communists and that he no longer saw any reason to appear to be supporting subversives by withholding "information." Victor Navasky, the publisher and editorial director of *The Nation*, wrote in his book about the blacklist, *Naming Names*, that when Arthur Miller sent a completed manuscript of *The Crucible* to Kazan, the director responded by saying that he would be honored to stage such a powerful new work. Miller is reported to have written back: "I didn't send it to you because I wanted you to direct it. I sent it to you because I want you to know what I think of stool-pigeons." "A man doesn't have to be an informer," Miller said at the time, "in order to practice his profession in the United States." In later years he admitted, however, that it was "a lot easier" for him than it was for friends like Kazan who were theater practitioners, since as a writer he could always go off and work by himself.

Jed Harris was the director of *The Crucible* when the play opened in Manhattan and received mixed reviews. "Simply because most people wouldn't know what a crucible was," Miller told Mel Gussow in 1996, "Jed thought it was a great title." The playwright said he made a list of twenty possible titles and thought if he called it *The Crucible* "they would all faint dead away." He explained the choice by saying that he "wanted something that would indicate the burning away of impurities, which is what the play does." The 1956 French film version, nevertheless, starring Yves Montand and Simone Signoret, was called *The Witches of Salem*. Miller said that the "Marxist" screenplay by Jean-Paul Sartre "shifted everything so that the rich peasants were persecuting the poor ones, and they were all Catholics. There were crucifixes inside all the houses. The whole thing was an absurdity, but there were some wonderful actors in it."

Robert Miller was the co-producer of the $25 million Hollywood version of the play, an Academy Award nominee released in 1996 by

Miller's future son-in-law Daniel Day-Lewis as John Proctor in Nicholas Hytner's 1996 film of *The Crucible*

Twentieth Century Fox. This was a big break for the playwright's son, a director of television commercials who had worked previously as a production assistant on *Midnight Cowboy* and *The Producers*, among other films. The younger Miller, who spent several rebellious years living in communes in California and Oregon, remarked that this was also a rare opportunity to renew their father-son relationship, which had "somehow remained the same," frozen in time since, as Robert said, "I was 21." For this project, which was shot on weather-beaten Hog Island, near Salem itself, Arthur Miller wrote his own screenplay, which was directed by Nicholas Hytner. The cast included Paul Scofield as Danforth, Winona Ryder as Abigail and Joan Allen, who had previously played Ann Deever in Jack O'Brien's production of *All My Sons*, as an austere Elizabeth Proctor. Daniel Day-Lewis was the doomed John

Proctor, a lean, proud, independent spirit, whose rugged individualism barely contained a mournful guilt that could not be assuaged. On the set the actor met Rebecca Miller, who accompanied her father; they were married soon after the movie was completed.

The play has also been adapted as an opera. Robert Ward's version, first performed at the New York City Opera in 1961, was revived in 1988 by the Juilliard School of Music, where it was conducted by John DeMain. More recently the work has been staged by the intimate Dicapo Opera Theater.

The most important thing about John Proctor, Miller observed, is that he is not meant to be heroic. He is simply "a damaged man" who rises against injustice. Louis Marks's highly effective 1982 production for BBC television placed this aspect of the work in sharp relief by casting Michael N. Harbour, a strong but relatively unknown actor, in the principal role. (The producer, anxious to hear the playwright's reaction, arranged for a special showing of the tape. The staff gathered around Miller, hanging on his every word, but he merely said, "It's really a very, very good play.") Yet it is naturally in the theater that the persuasiveness of Miller's through-line emerges with its full integrity. He spoke highly of Laurence Olivier's famous 1965 National Theatre production at the Old Vic, starring Colin Blakely and Joyce Redman. But he equally relished a performance he saw in Tbilisi, in former Soviet Georgia, where John Proctor, sporting a wide mustache, wore seventeenth-century Turkish pantaloons and was chased through the forest by a crowd waving scimitars.

*The Crucible* was the inaugural production when the Long Wharf Theatre opened in New Haven in 1964; Arvin Brown also presented it there twenty-five years later, starring Maryann Plunkett and Frank Converse. In 1989 there were two new interpretations of *The Crucible* running in Glasgow in the same season, one by a young Russian company, and the other in German by the Schiller Theater of Berlin. The play, of course, is frequently performed by regional theaters throughout the United States: there were memorable revivals by the Trinity

Repertory Company in Providence, Rhode Island in 1986, and in 1990 by the Roundabout Theatre Company in New York, where the show was directed by Gerald Freedman. The same year Howard Davies mounted the National Theatre's third London production. (Earlier performances had been staged in 1965 and 1980.) Michael Bryant, Oliver Cotton, Clare Holman and Paul Shelley were in his cast, but it was Zoe Wanamaker, sharing the Olivier Theatre stage with Tom Wilkinson, who revealed a new dimension to the personal dynamics of the drama. Here Elizabeth and John Proctor, two fundamentally decent people, were also fundamentally the wrong people for one another; the love they were capable of they simply could not offer to one another. Liam Neeson played John Proctor in a major Broadway production of *The Crucible* directed by Richard Eyre in 2002. Reviewing Neeson's performance in the *New Yorker*, John Lahr called him "a force of nature," so "absolutely rooted" was he "in the play's imaginative soil—a potent amalgam of sinew and sensitivity." Beneath the gloom of Paul Gallo's "crepuscular" lighting, Eyre emphasized both situation and Proctor's character, never releasing the audience from the trajectory of impending doom. "I have to admit," Miller said in 1989, "that it [feels] marvelous that McCarthy [is] what's-his-name while *The Crucible* is *The Crucible* still." "Not many people alive today may remember a lot about McCarthy," Miller added at the turn of the century. "But I hope they still remember something about my play. *The Crucible* has outlived him."

Not all of Miller's contemporaries bought the analogy *The Crucible* made between the Salem witch-hunt and the McCarthy show trials. The Communists were real, Frances Rudge (Kazan's third wife) protested, while the witches never existed. In the playwright's updating of what the Puritans called "the breaking of charity with one another" there was certainly no room for those who abhorred McCarthy's tactics but were equally horrified by the threat Stalin's outrages posed to the very idea of a liberal and humane democratic system. In a postscript to *Scoundrel Time* (1979) Lillian Hellman would have none of this: "I never want to live again to watch people turn into liars and cowards and

following pages   Liam Neeson (far left) as John Proctor in the 2002 Broadway production of *The Crucible*

others into frightened, silent collaborators. And to hell with the fancy reasons they give for what they did." In this regard the play has come to emblematize its period, both in its Cold War politics and pieties, but also in its passionate provocation. Danforth, moreover, as the play's chief interrogator, delivers a pivotal speech so full of menace that it is absolutely chilling in its contemporary implications: "You must understand, sir, a person is either with this Court or against it; there be no road between. This is a new time, a precise time; we live no longer in the dusky afternoon when evil mixed itself with good and befuddled the world. Now, by God's grace, the good folk and the evil entirely separate! I hope you will find your place with us." The great strength of a play like *The Crucible* is the way it liberates its audience from the merely literal. Any threat to entrenched authority at the moment when society is in transition, as Salem surely is in Miller's play, will find its scapegoats. This quintessentially American play does so tellingly, by casting "black magic" in the form of the predictably dark-skinned Tituba, the slave who was born in Barbados. In this monumental work Miller shows us that the outsider we fear most lies hidden deep within ourselves. The greatest threat of all is our ability to be so easily seduced not by the Devil, but by the lure of power in the crucible of tyranny: one of Proctor's principal accusers merely wants his land. "The artist's powerful desire," Miller wrote, "to penetrate life's chaos, to make it meaningfully cohere, has literally created a truth as substantial as a sword for later generations to wield against their own oppression."

Although Miller had been taken off-guard by some of the initial reactions to *Death of a Salesman* in 1949—he turned down an offer by a prominent company to present a series of lectures to their marketing staff on how to avoid the mistakes Willy Loman made during his lackluster career—no such misunderstandings greeted the appearance of *The Crucible* four years later. The point of this play was, if anything, almost too clear, especially to those Cold Warriors determined to manipulate public opinion. In 1954 the State Department denied Miller's application for a passport to attend the Brussels premiere of the play. When the Belgian audience cried out "author, author!" at the conclusion of the first night performance, the U.S. Ambassador took the stage instead. "It didn't harm me," the playwright told *Newsweek* magazine, "It harmed the country." But by that time Miller was involved in another, more personal crisis: his 16-year marriage to Mary Slattery was full of "anger and tension" and he had become increasingly involved with the actress Marilyn Monroe.

In 1996 Robert Miller told Stephen Farber in the *New York Times* that he hadn't understood until he was working with the crew filming *The Crucible* how much the play's sexual tension and Proctor's guilt over infidelity reflected his father's emotional state during the time he was writing the play. "When I started work on the film and reacquainted myself with the play," Robert said, "I realized from where Arthur had drawn those dynamics. I was very moved by the scenes about betrayal and forgiveness in a marriage." The playwright had actually met the movie star several times during the early 1950s, and "he wrote *The Crucible* during the period when he began to fall under her spell." They were an unlikely couple: he the tall, handsome, socially engaged, intellectual writer, she the vivacious, role-playing, peroxide Hollywood bombshell of *How to Marry a Millionaire*, *The Prince and the Showgirl*, *The Seven Year Itch* and *Some Like It Hot*. For many years, Miller was reluctant to talk in public about this relationship, especially after the reactions to the original production of *After the Fall* in 1964. But he did so in 1990, when his autobiography appeared in his seventy-fifth year. Though too many writers (including Norman Mailer, Philip Roth, Joyce Carol Oates and Gloria Steinem) have fantasized, even fetishized the circumstances that brought this high-profile couple together in public—New York Jewish boy-made-good marries shiksa above all other shiksas—in *Timebends* Miller relies on a candor and self-reflection that has the ring of truth. Soon after completing the autobiography he said: "in the end, I simply fell in love." (He was somewhat more guarded, however, in the interviews he gave at the time.) His version of the Monroe years has nevertheless failed to satisfy the Marilyn-mythologizers, who continue to read it as self-serving.

Miller married Marilyn Monroe in 1956. As Martin Gottfried reports, there were two wedding ceremonies. The first took place quietly in the Westchester County Court House in White Plains, New York, when the couple tried to elude the paparazzi. Reporters chasing them in the car driven by Miller's cousin Morton skidded off the road; one died. Marilyn took this as a bad omen. Two days later, on July 1, they had a traditional Jewish wedding in Katonah, New York. The double-ring ceremony (the bride wore beige) was attended by the play-wright's parents, his children, close family and a few friends, including Lee and Paula Strasberg, Norman and Edna Rosten, Miller's sister Joan and her husband George Kupchik, and his brother Kermit and wife Frances. The star converted to Judaism; Miller never took this seriously, while Marilyn apparently did. She told one friend that she "wanted to be closer to Arthur." Both had to wait more than a year for their previous marriages to be dissolved. Hers to Joe DiMaggio was a physically abusive relationship, though for almost forty years the baseball hero would religiously place a single rose on her grave to mark the anniversary of her death. (The veteran New York Yankee died in California in 2001.) Miller's divorce was expensive. Mary Miller was awarded custody of their two children, Jane (b. 1944) and Robert (b. 1947), child support payments (including rises in the cost of living), the house they had recently bought on Willow Street in Brooklyn Heights, plus a percentage of all his future earnings until she remarried (she never did).

In the early months of Monroe's marriage to Miller, when she lived with the playwright in his modest farmhouse in Roxbury, Connecticut, she was desperate to have a child. She suffered a miscarriage, though her public only glimpsed pictures of a buxom body and a smiling face. A few months before their wedding Miller was summoned before the House Committee on Un-American Activities. After three years, McCarthy's demagogues were losing some of their initial fire, and they needed something—and someone—to put them back on the front page.

Marilyn Monroe and Arthur Miller shortly after their marriage, July 1956

Miller testifying before the House Committee on Un-American Activities, June 21, 1956

In 1956, with Marilyn at the height of her fame, the playwright was an irresistible target; the committee probably knew in advance that he would refuse to name names. Representative Francis Waters, the committee chairman, let the playwright know that things might go a lot easier for him if he could persuade his fiancée to pose for a campaign photograph with him. The couple declined his offer. A year later Miller was cited for contempt, though he received no penalty and his passport was renewed. On the steps of the United States Congress with the glamorous Marilyn on his arm—an improbable photo op if ever there was one—Miller stood his ground; he vowed to have his case heard on appeal. In 1958 he was elected to the National Institute of Arts and Letters, and the Supreme Court unanimously overturned his conviction for contempt of Congress. Marilyn Monroe had previously bought every member of the Senate and the House of Representatives a subscription to *I.F. Stone's Weekly*, a major progressive forum whose very existence depended on the right of free speech.

In spite of so much turmoil in his life, Miller produced two new plays. *A Memory of Two Mondays* and a one-act version of *A View from the Bridge*, in which the narrator spoke in blank verse, were presented on a double bill in 1955 for a short run in New York. The next year Peter Brook directed Miller's revised, two-act version of *A View from the Bridge* at the Comedy Theatre in London, starring Anthony Quayle; in 1958, when Brook brought his production to Paris, Raf Vallone led the cast. By that time, Luchino Visconti's *Uno Squardo dal Ponte*, interpreted through the cinematographer's neo-realistic techniques, was a huge box-office success in Italy. In developing the scope and social milieu of the drama, Miller's new script omitted Alfieri's verse dialogue and, in order to give the work more psychological depth, greatly expanded the two major parts for women—Beatrice, Eddie Carbone's wife, and her 17-year-old niece, Catherine.

Miller had been thinking of writing a play about Sicilian-Americans as far back as the late 1940s. In a notebook he kept while working on

J. Carrol Naish in the 1955 production of *A Memory of Two Mondays*

the ideas and language he might use for the script that became *Death of a Salesman*, he jotted down a memo to himself to write "the Italian play [about X] who ratted on the two immigrants." Nor was the setting for this play, Red Hook, entirely new territory for him. In 1951 he abandoned a filmscript called *The Hook*, which had been sold to Harry Cohn at Columbia Pictures. Set in the shadow of the Brooklyn Bridge, the scenario dealt with corrupt union leadership in league with the Mafia, and the threat of wildcat strikes by longshoremen working on the docks and living in and around Carroll Street. Miller and Kazan took the train to Los Angeles to consult with Cohn about the project; while in

Mary Ure and Anthony Quayle rehearsing a scene from *A View from the Bridge*, performed at the Comedy Theatre, London, 1956

California both met Marilyn Monroe for the first time. In the middle of the Red Scare, Columbia Pictures wanted to add an anti-Communist element to the mix. Cohn felt that this property, and Miller's muckraking angle on it, was too hot to handle, though Hollywood did produce another, highly successful movie dealing with some of the same material: *On the Waterfront*, with Marlon Brando. In that film, a Budd Schulberg-Elia Kazan collaboration set in Hoboken, New Jersey's Red Hook counterpart, the informer stands justified. "We're members of history," Miller reflected, looking back at this episode in his life. "Some of us don't know it, but you better learn it for your own preservation."

*A View from the Bridge* is a play about betrayal, both personal and tribal. Eddie Carbone lies to himself, to Beatrice and to the lawyer Alfieri long before he lets the immigration authorities know about the "submarine" status of Beatrice's cousins Marco and Rodolpho. Eddie's act of betrayal seals their fate but so, too, does it certify him as a modern tragic figure caught in the web of a highly unstable social reality. Miller looked for the essence of tragedy in the life of "the common man"; he found it in the figure of Eddie Carbone. "Modern drama," the playwright said, "has lost the ability to deal with the whole man. What is needed is a new social drama which will combine the approach of the Greek theatre with modern discoveries in psychology and economics." To make this synthesis work on stage, Miller adapted a number of devices from the classical Greek theater. Foremost among these is the ambiguous role he assigns to Alfieri, who serves as both choral commentator and protagonist as the play's rising action leads to retribution and the finality of death. "The secret of the Greek drama is the vendetta, the family ties incomprehensible to Englishmen and Americans. But not to Jews." As narrator, Alfieri's job is to frame the scene, nostalgically, in the full context of tragic inevitability. The prologue he speaks reminds us that the story he is about to tell could have taken place just as fatefully in another time and in some other, distant place: "This is Red Hook, not Sicily. This is the slum that faces the seaward side of the Brooklyn Bridge…in Calabria perhaps or on the cliff at Syracuse, another lawyer quite differently dressed, heard the same complaint and sat there as powerless as I, and watched it run its bloody course." But Alfieri, who has no scenes with anyone else but Carbone, is also his would-be confessor: wounded, conflicted and hurting, the longshoreman returns to the lawyer's office several times as catastrophe looms so relentlessly. Eddie has nowhere else to go. The disquieting series of duets reveals Eddie's growing but unacknowledged sexual passion for his teenage niece. The odd snatches of lyrics from the old pop-tune, "Paper Doll"—"I want to buy a paper doll that I can call my own"—serve to ironize, then intensify, Eddie's despair. When Alfieri confronts him, urging him to "let her go" because he cannot marry Catherine himself—coming too near the truth—Eddie cuts him off with an abruptness that nonetheless tells the whole story: "What the hell are you talking about!" Miller has "the dramatist's gift for making even the most inarticulate characters eloquent," the director Nicholas Hytner once observed. Eddie speaks the rough language of a dockworker; the playwright allows his subtext to fall elsewhere. As Miller noted, "Once Eddie had been squarely placed in his social context, among his people, the mythlike feeling of the story emerged of itself."

Outside of the artificial device of the chorus, Alfieri, the reasoner, the intellectual and the man with a view from the bridge, is not the only character to feel the impending sense of doom. Beatrice, intuitively at first, slowly but deliberately charts the course of her husband's bitter downfall; yet she is powerless in the face of forces she tries to understand but which remain beyond her control. "The truth is not as bad as blood, Eddie!" she tries to warn her husband in a moment of spectacular dramatic foreshadowing. She knows, too, that Catherine must marry Marco's brother Rodolpho, the young, blond Sicilian who likes to sing and cook and sew. Eddie, who has long been absent from Beatrice's bed, is threatened by more than a potential rival. The very qualities that mark the lithe Rodolpho with a different kind of masculinity are also the attributes that make him a disturbing subject of homoerotic desire. "He's like weird," Eddie remarks. "And with that whacky hair; he's like a chorus girl or sup'm." Eddie's secure place in the only world he knows begins to slip, fatally, when he reaches out to Catherine's lover and kisses him on the mouth. Shocked and confused—he has reacted passionately, not logically—he runs offstage to betray Beatrice's cousins as the illegal "aliens" they are.

This is a stunning psychological portrait, yet one conceived within a vibrant, colorful and sometimes dangerous working-class world. In a neighborhood lined with clapboard houses divided into apartments cheek by jowl, and where fire escapes serve as balconies that are also windows to the world, street life is vital. An old-world Roman

Catholicism is writ large, as is the Mediterranean vendetta and the code of honor. Miller relied for local color on the trip he made in 1947 to Palermo and Catania with his friends Vincent James ("Vinny") Longhi and Mitch Berenson, who tried to keep alive the work of Pete Panto, a young firebrand executed gangland-style for challenging the leadership of Joseph Frank, then head of the International Longshoremen's Association. In Sicily the playwright also met the celebrity gangster Lucky Luciano. Red Hook's ties to corruption ran deep.

In *A View from the Bridge* Marco challenges his betrayer; Eddie dies when the knife he holds in his hand is twisted into his own heart. Everybody in this transplanted world speaks the same language, and revenge is a ceremony performed for the entire community. The ritual has to end in death. And everybody knows everybody else's business; one's responsibility (always a key word for Miller) is to group identity and group solidarity. "Submarines" are hidden everywhere; you just don't "rat" on your own. When you betray "the other" in your neighbor, you betray "the other" in yourself. That is why Alfieri, in the closing lines of the play—an epilogue really—will always mourn Eddie "with a certain…alarm." "Much that has been interpreted in lofty terms, fate, religion, etc.," Miller observed, "is only blood and tribal survival within the family. Red Hook is full of Greek tragedies."

*A View from the Bridge* is also the play in the Miller canon that has grown most in stature since its original one-act version was greeted with lukewarm reviews by the New York press. Although the work as we know it today did not appear in the United States until 1965, in an off-Broadway production starring Robert Duvall and Jon Voight that ran for 780 performances, Sidney Lumet's 1962 film with Maureen Stapleton, Raf Vallone and a young Carol Lawrence, based on an adaptation by Norman Rosten, already suggested the story's potential for the performance of ethnicity, machismo and forbidden sexuality. In 1987 the British actor Michael Gambon scored one of the great successes of his career with a powerful interpretation of the play's lead role at the National Theatre in London. Directed by Alan Ayckbourn in the

Miller with Raf Vallone and Carol Lawrence during the making of Sidney Lumet's 1962 film of *A View from the Bridge*

Michael Gambon with Elizabeth Bell and Suzan Sylvester in the 1987 production
of *A View from the Bridge* at the Cottesloe Theatre in London

intimate space of the Cottesloe Theatre, the cast also featured an intense and clear-sighted James Hayes in the difficult role of Alfieri. For this production the all-British company, working with the dialect coach Joan Washington, made the wise choice of forgoing authenticity in the sound of the play's language. In its place they created a stage Italian-American Brooklynese that, as Miller noted, never interfered with his vision of the play. "The actors spoke in a rhythm which had absolutely nothing to do with the naturalistic rhythm of speech," the playwright said. "The play was spoken like music, fast and slow according to considerations other than the customary way of saying those lines. It was done in accents which don't exist on heaven or earth because they didn't know the New York Italian accent. But it was terrific, marvelous." A muscular Anthony LaPaglia, who had starred as Mangiacavallo in a much-acclaimed revival of *The Rose Tattoo* two years before at the Circle in the Square, played Eddie in 1997 to much critical acclaim at the Criterion Center for the Roundabout Theatre Company in New York. Allison Janney's Beatrice was his precise counterpart, a mixture of backbone, frustrated sexuality, growing comprehension and foreboding. Stephen Spinella was a ghost-like Alfieri. Using David Gallo's unit set, defined by four freestanding staircases and a painted backdrop of the skeletal cranes and hoists of the waterfront, the director Michael Mayer employed a large cast of extras in the amphitheater to create a sense of the crowded, bustling but always vulnerable community Eddie ultimately betrays. "However much one might dislike this man, who does all sorts of frightful things," Miller said, "he possesses and exemplifies the wondrous and humane fact that he too can be driven to what in the last analysis is a sacrifice of himself for his conception, however misguided, of right, dignity and justice."

The stage life of this play continues to have other interpretations, just as revealing. Sebastiano Lo Monaco was the first Sicilian actor to play Eddie Carbone in a production for the Teatro di Messina staged by Giuseppe Patroni Griffi in 2003–4. The version of "Paper Doll" used was Louis Prima's. Gerardo Guerrieri's Italian translation deftly substituted pungent Americanisms for the original's Sicilian patina, turning the play inside-out. With the playwright's permission, Darryl V. Jones transposed the site from 1950s Italian Red Hook to the contemporary world of Dominican immigrants in Queens, New York in an adaptation that worked with surprising immediacy and clarity. "As Eddie Carbone blindly propels himself on a path of vengeance," the director said, "all that is American fails him. Eddie sinks deeper into an abyss of obsession where a call for justice and Old World passions arise. Blood for blood."

*A View from the Bridge* has also been staged as an opera in two different versions, the first completed as early as 1961. The second, with a libretto written by Arnold Weinstein and the playwright himself, was William Bolcom's musically accomplished work, scored for 13 soloists, a 48-member chorus and an orchestra of 75, which had its world premiere at the Lyric Opera of Chicago on October 9, 1999. Directed by Frank Galati, with set and costume design by Santo Loquasto, the soprano Catherine Malfitano sang the role of Beatrice, accompanied by Kim Josephson as Eddie and Timothy Nolen as the attorney Alfieri. In 2002 the Lyric's arresting production was also performed at the Metropolitan Opera House at Lincoln Center in New York. Miller always said that *A View from the Bridge* was his most "operatic" play. As Anthony Tommasini wrote in the *New York Times*, "the story could be a modern-day Verdi tragedy."

In the early part of their six-year relationship, Miller and Monroe seemed to have been, on the surface at least, mutually supportive. She stood by him when he defied the House Committee on Un-American Activities; he traveled with her to attend the British premiere of *The Prince and the Showgirl* in London, where he met her famous co-star, Laurence Olivier. He also wrote scenes for her picture with Yves Montand, *Let's Make Love*, released in 1960. Miller was convinced that the Hollywood studio system exploited his wife by contracting her to present repetitive, sexualized images of herself, both on screen and off

Gregory Turay as Rodolpho (foreground) with Mark McCrory as Marco, Catherine Malfitano as Beatrice, Juliana Rambaldi as Catherine and Kim Josephson as Eddie Carbone in the world premiere of the William Bolcom opera of *A View from the Bridge* at the Lyric Opera of Chicago, 1999

(the word Miller used was "silly"). Monroe, on her part, played to the camera well; a master of comic timing, she took full advantage of its power to transform her being, and especially her body, from plain Norma Jean Baker into the allure of one of the world's great superstars. But her real talent as an actress, Miller believed, lay elsewhere. He wrote *The Misfits*, according to the actor Eli Wallach, as a "valentine" to his wife; yet her haunting performance as the fragile and tormented Roslyn in what was to be her last appearance on screen offered her audience an image of Monroe they had never seen before.

Miller called *The Misfits* "an Eastern western." He described its subject as "people trying to connect and unable to connect," people with "an unrequited longing for something they couldn't name." What is on display here is "the displacement in life of commitment." The character Monroe plays in the film had a previous incarnation in a short story of the same name. In that narrative Roslyn Taber, a character who never appears, is a schoolteacher who has arrived in Reno seeking a divorce. Ironically, the playwright discovered Nevada while divorcing his first wife so that he could marry Monroe. For the screenplay Miller greatly expanded the offstage role of Roslyn, the "saddest girl in the world." "If I'm going to be alone," she points out to her ex, "I want to be alone by myself." The dialogue Miller wrote for her is rich, full of poignancy and punch. "I don't know where I belong," she admits to Gay, the ageing cowboy twice her age with whom she forms a tentative romantic alliance. Later she tells him, "Maybe all there really is is what happens next, just the next thing," before her voice trails off in silence. Just like the wild horses the cowboys chase, mustangs too small for rodeo or ranch work and thus fated to be ground up for dog food, all the characters in Miller's screenplay are "misfits."

John Huston directed the 124-minute, black-and-white movie based on Miller's film script, with a highly atmospheric soundtrack by Alex North. On-location shots were filmed in Reno and Dayton, Nevada, sometimes in 100°F weather. This was to be Clark Gable's last movie, too. Miller said the "casting of Gable was a problem, because while he was intrigued by the script, he didn't understand it. It had him completely mixed up as to what kind of a film this really was going to be." Gable, who observed only that the piece was set in the West and that his character was a cowboy, nonetheless turned in a fully developed performance as Gay Langland, the unattached philanderer who used to be such a dark-haired heart-throb. He now works overtime to mask what he knows is the emptiness of a life that has passed him by. The actor performed all the stunts the role demanded, including bronco-busting, but he never saw the finished piece. He died of a heart attack on November 16, 1960 at the age of 59, just eight days before the film was completed. *The Misfits* also featured a third movie legend, Montgomery Clift, in the role of the sensitive Perce Howland, the over-the-hill and psychologically scarred former rodeo star. His big scene takes place in a phone booth in the middle of nowhere. There was a strong supporting cast, including Eli Wallach as Guido, another cowboy who makes a play for Roslyn, and Thelma Ritter as Isabelle Steers, landlady, hard drinker and wistful romancer of better days.

Tony Huston, the director's son, said that although his father's dynamic presence usually "loomed large on any set," *The Misfits* was really an Arthur Miller film. The playwright traveled to the hot Nevada desert to be with Marilyn for the recording of scenes on-location; but as the project slowly progressed, it became clear that his marriage had seriously deteriorated ("personally," Tony Huston said, "it was terrible"). Angela Allen, the script supervisor, remembers the playwright arriving "absolutely besotted" with Monroe; looking back, however, she remarked that what she really watched was "the disintegration of a marriage." Jones Schoenburg of Magnum, which had exclusive rights to do the still photography, felt that "there was a tremendous amount of tension. It was an anxious set." Everyone knew that Monroe had just had an affair with the French actor Yves Montand, and her behavior during the shoot was compromised by drug dependency, including one overdose. "She'd walk on the set" hours late and "nobody said a word,"

Montgomery Clift, Marilyn Monroe
and Clark Gable in the 1961 film,
*The Misfits*, written by Arthur Miller

recalls Edward Parone, assistant to the neophyte producer Frank E. Taylor, who had published Miller in 1944 when he was an editor in the firm of Reynal & Hitchcock. In addition to being late for scene calls, or missing them completely, Monroe had trouble remembering her lines and increasingly fell under the troubling influence of Paula Strasberg, who was eventually barred from the set on John Huston's insistence. "If you see the movie closely," Eli Wallach noted, "you will see how vulnerable, how unhappy she was."

"Marilyn was highly self-destructive," Miller told a French newspaper in 1992. "All of my energy and attention were devoted to trying to help her solve her problems. Unfortunately, I didn't have much success." The couple divorced in 1961, just before *The Misfits* was released. Monroe's final comment on the end of her four-and-a-half-year marriage to Miller is reported to have been, "I think he's a better writer than a husband."

One of the Magnum photographers sent to Nevada to take stills of *The Misfits* was the Austrian-born photojournalist Inge Morath. She was at first apprehensive about meeting such a "serious author as Arthur Miller"; her knowledge of his work was limited to only one play, *Death of a Salesman*. But here he was right in front of her, floating on his back in a swimming pool, smoking a cigar and telling jokes to John Huston. "He was a great storyteller," Morath said. Miller had "no time for her on the set," but some months later they met again through mutual friends in New York. They were married in Connecticut on February 17, 1962 when Morath was 38, and quickly set about having two children. Daniel was born the same year with Down's Syndrome; at birth he was placed in a home where his mother saw him regularly. He has lived for many years at the Southbury Training School, a facility for "the developmentally disabled" near the family home in Roxbury. His father did not mention him in *Timebends*, nor did his name appear in the official biography of either parent. (According to the playwright's sister, "Daniel was a very difficult subject for Arthur.") Their second child, Rebecca Augusta, born a year later, has had an accomplished career as

Arthur Miller (center) with the producer Frank E. Taylor and the actor Clark Gable, on the set of *The Misfits*, Nevada, 1960

an actress, screenwriter and film director. When she was thirteen she converted to Catholicism. "My father," she said, "wasn't happy," though as a young adult she became as secular as her parents; "just another confused person." At Yale her roommate was the actress Jodie Foster; she now lives with her husband, Daniel Day-Lewis, and their children, mostly in Ireland. As a young actress she appeared in Peter Brook's production of *The Cherry Orchard* at the Brooklyn Academy of Music. (One of Norman Mailer's daughters was also in the cast.) Her film credits include roles in *Consenting Adults, Mrs. Parker and the Vicious Circle*, the 1994 version of *Love Affair* starring Warren Beatty and Mike Nichols's *Regarding Henry*. In 1995 her film *Angela* was a prizewinner at the Sundance Festival, and in 2002 she was the screenwriter-director of the well-received *Personal Velocity*, based on three of her short stories. Her other film credits include the very affecting father-daughter relationship portrayed in *The Ballad of Jack and Rose*, released in 2005 and starring Day-Lewis. On March 24, 2005 she told Terry Gross on National Public Radio that she was writing a screenplay based on *The Man Who Had All the Luck*. It was "a way of spending more time with my dad when he was sick."

Miller's third marriage was an enduring one, lasting forty years. Inge Morath, who died on January 30, 2002 from lymphatic cancer, was born in Graz on May 27, 1923. What attracted her to Miller, she said, was "the integrity of his mind." Her parents were scientists who moved to Nazi Germany where, as a teenager, she was sent to the forced labor camp at Tempelhof for refusing to join the Hitler Youth. Martin Gottfried reports that two of her brothers fought in the Wehrmacht, the regular German army, in which their uncle held the rank of general. After she graduated from Berlin University in 1944, she did her obligatory wartime work in an aircraft factory and performing what she later called menial "labor service." When the war was over, she was hired as an interpreter for the U.S. Information Services. Morath moved to France in 1950: when her previous short marriage ended in divorce she went to work with the Austrian photographers Ernst Haas and Erich Lessing.

Arthur Miller and Inge Morath on their wedding day, February 17, 1962

After the successful publication of her photo-essay on French worker priests, Robert Capa invited her to join the Magnum collective in 1955, where she initially worked as an assistant to Henri Cartier-Bresson. Morath's several projects in collaboration with her husband include *In Russia* (1969), *In the Country* (1977), *Chinese Encounters* (1979) and *Salesman in Beijing* (1984); she was also well-known for her witty photographs of masks made by their friend Saul Steinberg. (After Morath's death, Miller's companion was Agnes Barley, a painter born in Jacksonville, Florida in 1970. At the playwright's home in Roxbury they worked in adjacent studios; Barley inherited Miller's apartment in New York when he died.)

Miller wrote two important plays during the first years of his marriage to Inge Morath, *Incident at Vichy* and *After the Fall*. Both appeared first in New York in 1964, and both reveal the playwright's difficulty in using the Holocaust as material for dramatic representation. This was a problem that would plague him in the series of works that also includes *Playing for Time* and *Broken Glass*. The short play Miller set in Vichy, France followed the premiere of *After the Fall* by only eleven months. From a structural point of view it may be the easiest of these plays to understand, for though it aims to hold the stage with authority its shape is really that of a theatricalized moral debate. Miller based this work on an actual story told to him by a former psychoanalyst, a survivor who had been picked up by the Gestapo for carrying false papers and who had been saved from the extermination camps by someone he had never seen before. An unknown individual had simply stepped forward and substituted himself in the line-up of "suspected" Jewish men waiting to have their circumcised penises inspected. Miller also based the pivotal figure of Von Berg on his wife's close Austrian friend, Prince Josef von Schwarzenberg, who had refused to cooperate with the Nazis and had suffered the consequences. *Incident at Vichy* highlights the contrast between the cynical psychoanalyst, Leduc, who knows that he is doomed, and the idealistic but unproven Von Berg, who still clings to the efficacy of a noble set of beliefs, despite all evidence to the contrary.

Ira Lewis, Joseph Wiseman, Will Lee, David Stewart, David Wayne, Michael Strong and Stanley Beck in the 1964 production of *Incident at Vichy* in New York

"Jew is only the name we give to that stranger," Leduc argues, "that agony we cannot feel, that death we look at like a cold abstraction. Each man has his Jew; the black, the yellow, the white, it is the other. And the Jews have their Jews."

Miller introduces a third character into their debate, the German major who finally admits in an outburst of self-revelation that he is merely doing his job: "There are no persons anymore, don't you see that? There will never be persons again. What do I care if you love me? Are you out of your mind? What am I, a dog that I must be loved? You…goddamned Jews!" So much, Leduc concludes, for humanity. But before he gives up on it completely, Leduc must make Von Berg understand exactly where "complicity" lies: in Von Berg's simple relief in knowing that history has determined that it is not his turn to play "the Jew." Leduc's challenge is as caustic as it is revelatory: "It's not your guilt I want, it's your responsibility."

In the historical context that is the real engine for this play, "decency" is meaningless without risk and without the effective advocacy of action. As the play ends, when the Nazi major stares with cold calculation at the moral aristocrat's face—they remain "forever incomprehensible to one another, looking into each other's eyes"—it is the unwitting Leduc who learns the most fateful lesson. Von Berg forfeits his "pass" and gives Leduc a way out the open door. "I wasn't asking you to do this!" Leduc cries out, "You don't owe me this!" Now the guilt will be the psychoanalyst's: the guilt of the survivor. Heroism is pretty much beside the point.

Miller's incorporation of other Jewish characters into this "incident," all of whom will be murdered in the gas chambers, serves to advance, nonetheless, the force of Leduc's argument about guilt (moral but passive) and responsibility (ethical and active). Lebeau, an accomplished painter, places his faith in art and the imagination; the electrician Bayard, a Marxist, sees the horror of anti-Semitism as yet another tool for the exploitation of the masses; Monceau, an actor, believes that he can defy the ugly reality that awaits him by pretending that he is only playing a part in someone else's drama. All are equally deluded. Miller assigns symbolic actions to two other figures in an attempt to emblematize their communal fate. Relying on a well-worn theatrical device (it appears, not insignificantly, in *The Merchant of Venice*), the exchange of rings makes us see that these men will die simply because they are Jews. A young boy takes a ring off his finger and presses it into Leduc's hands. Give it to my mother, he implores; tell her to remember me. The Old Jew carries his bedding, the last vestige of a portable home. When it rips open just before he is called into the antechamber where his fate is to be sealed, silence arrests the dramatic action. Feathers overwhelm the stage. At Auschwitz, too, and soon, this old man will disappear into thin air.

Harold Clurman's original New York production, starring Hal Holbrook and Joseph Wiseman, never fully succeeded in finding the play beneath Miller's compelling debate. Stacy Keach's 1973 television adaptation, with Harris Yulin as a thoroughly convincing and conflicted Leduc, took great advantage of its eighty minutes on the small screen to emphasize the hothouse atmosphere of this one-set drama, where history and the politics of anti-Semitism continue to have a curious way of upstaging the actors. *Incident at Vichy* was the first of Miller's plays to be banned in the Soviet Union. Beginning with the anti-Jewish push in the 1960s, the play was not to be seen there for nineteen years. (In 1970, in response to *In Russia*, all of Miller's works were similarly placed on the index of censorship.) And when the playwright attacked the Soviets for their suppression of free speech and their continuing anti-Semitism in the 1980s, after the ban on his work was supposedly lifted, they closed down Galina Volchek's production of the play. French producers, nervous about the play's reception in light of their country's collaboration with the Nazis in the systematic round-up of Jews, their fellow citizens, turned their backs on this work. When Pierre Cardin finally produced *Incident at Vichy* in Paris in the 1980s, it received bitter reviews.

The politics surrounding Miller's *After the Fall*, and the strong reaction the New York production provoked only two years after Marilyn Monroe's death at the age of thirty-six, were, if anything, even

Miller and Elia Kazan plan for Kazan's production of *After the Fall*, which premiered in New York in January 1964

more personal and intense. When Barbara Loden, the original Maggie, walked onto the set of the ANTA Washington Square Theatre wearing a blonde wig (Marilyn wore a platinum one in *The Misfits*), Miller and his director might have known they were asking for trouble. That director was none other than Elia Kazan; after a ten-year feud, the two had set aside their own ongoing dispute and resumed their legendary partnership. The Marilyn look-alike should have signaled even further alarm; it was well known in the industry that Kazan had had an affair with Monroe, and that at some point, before her marriage to Miller, she had probably been sleeping with both of them. None of these circumstances was made any easier by the fact that *After the Fall*, selected as the inaugural production for the new Lincoln Center for the Performing Arts, had to open downtown, an unhappy result of persistent cost overruns, labor disputes and construction delays.

Elia Kazan on the set of *After the Fall*, New York, 1963

Miller said that *After the Fall* was "not about Marilyn." For him the conflict pivoted, instead, on a different issue, of which the thinly disguised figure of his famous wife ("hardly the play's *raison d'être*") surely played its part: "Could anyone, in all truth, really save another unless that other wished to be saved?" The playwright had been asked to work on a screenplay based on Albert Camus' *The Fall*, and it is from that existential novel, not the "fall of man" (in the Christian interpretation of the expulsion from the Garden of Eden told in Genesis), that the drama takes its title. Miller had been struck by the shape Camus gave to his narrator's failure "to come to the aid of a girl he saw jump off a bridge into a river." A fictional character's call for help, and the uneasy conscience that results from "the iniquitous act of indifference," gave the playwright the seed image he had been looking for in what he hoped would be his own "concentration on ethics" and "the paradox of denial."

The script as written, however, is full of autobiographical refer-
ences—so many indeed that, especially in the original production, they
threatened to overtake whatever might have been the dramatist's philo-
sophical concerns during the two years he spent working on this project. Miller had been undergoing analysis for several years, and the play's
structure seems to reflect this introspective experience. *After the Fall* is
first and foremost a memory play. Everything takes place in "the mind,
thought and memory" of Quentin, the anguished, liberal lawyer we
meet in the play's opening scene. He is both narrator and observer of
the stage events as they idiosyncratically unfold. Quentin is also listen-
er, judge and jury. Everything is told from his point of view; this time
we are—literally—inside his head. What he details sounds, not surprisingly, familiar: two failed marriages, the most recent to a drugged-out
singer-performer; his reluctance to commit himself to a third marriage,
this time to the compassionate but nevertheless intellectually demanding German refugee Holga; a preoccupation with the ethical demeanor
of his friend Mickey, who is actually called before the House
Committee on Un-American Activities; unresolved conflicts with both
father and mother (Gussie Miller died on March 7, 1961); and above all
his impassioned debate with himself on questions of guilt, survival and
individual responsibility in post-Holocaust America. None of this is told
sequentially, as the play's structure, like that of *Death of a Salesman*, defies
any conventional notion of stage realism. Characters fade in and fade
out, depending on their necessary presence in the highly selective
memories Quentin stages and crafts in an attempt to make sense of the
muddle he has made of his own mid-life.

Whether or not *After the Fall* has the potential to rise above the
level of self-indulgence depends almost entirely on its ability to frame
the narrator's crisis within the tragic history of a much wider public
domain. "The complex process of denial in the great world reflected in
an individual seemed a wonderfully illuminating thematic center,"
Miller recalled in *Timebends*. Quentin's personal saga of betrayals
in *After the Fall* is played out in the shadow of a concentration camp

Miller with his wife Inge Morath and the children of his first marriage,
Jane and Robert, listening backstage to the intercom re-transmission
of *After the Fall*, New York, 1964

watchtower; and it is this aspect of Miller's dramatic design, perhaps even more than the exploitive Monroe retrospective, that continues to raise the most alarm. Miller was attacked for trivializing, perhaps even "relativizing" the Shoah by using it as background material for a self-aggrandizing tale of guilt and personal redemption. Like many others, Miller's brother Kermit found the play offensive; its attempt to show that all humanity shared the blame for the Holocaust, and not just the Germans, had the hideous effect of neutralizing Nazi genocide by "universalist" implication. "I was sure that the play would be seen as an attempt to embrace a world of political and ethical dilemmas," Miller wrote in 1987. "The play was about how we—nations and individuals—destroy ourselves by denying that this is precisely what we are doing."

The history of this play in production tells quite a different story. Robert Whitehead, the producer for the New York premiere, told Miller that "everyone would of course reduce Maggie to a portrait, purely and simply, of Marilyn Monroe." That has more or less been the show's fate. But just who was responsible for costuming Barbara Loden in a blonde wig (she became Elia Kazan's wife after Molly Thacher died), and the precedent this established for the interpretation of the role, is a subject about which the key players in the original production—playwright, director and company—were conspicuously silent. Jason Robards, cast as Quentin, was seen as the inevitable Miller stand-in, just as Monroe shadowed Maggie. Gilbert Cates may have made the same miscalculation when he cast Faye Dunaway and Christopher Plummer in his two-and-a-half-hour production for NBC, broadcast in December 1974. His static staging did little to expand the play's range of possibilities. It was not until 1990, when Michael Blakemore directed Josette Simon, an accomplished black British actress, in the part of Maggie that the play took on wider resonances. Although a South African production had previously toured England, Blakemore's National Theatre version, starring James Laurenson as Quentin and Henry Goodman as Mickey, was the work's long-delayed British premiere. When Miller agreed to a slight modification in Maggie's profile (Simon played her in a dark wig as a drug-dependent, sultry jazz singer), the race-blind casting finally liberated his play from the haunting image of Marilyn. "Halfway through the second act," the director said at the time, "the memory of Monroe goes out the window."

Elia Kazan's initial staging of *After the Fall* was plagued by additional problems. The open, arena-like space at ANTA made it impossible for actors to appear and disappear, as they are meant to do in Miller's script. Franco Zeffirelli's 1966 production in Rome was far more responsive to the work's dramatic structure. The Italian director employed a set built of steel frames "which gave the impression that one was looking into the back of a bellows camera." According to Janet N. Balakian, actors "could enter through openings in these covers and make their entrances and exits on the stage at any depth." Pneumatic lifts "silently and invisibly raised the actors so that they could appear and disappear instantaneously." Zeffirelli's deft rendition gave the audience the impression of being inside the narrator's head. Miller also praised Marcello Mastroianni's portrayal of Quentin. According to the playwright, who attended the Italian premiere, "he seemed to be trying to puzzle out what was happening to him while still regarding himself from a certain distance."

Hayden Griffin's set for Michael Blakemore's London production in the Olivier Theatre, reconfiguring one of the basic shapes of the universe, the golden mean spiral, ensured a similar fluidity and flexibility. Allowing figures from the past to materialize and dissolve with the speed of thought, its vanishing point connected with a watchtower at Quentin's moments of moral crisis. Miller's Indian director, meanwhile, told him that in his country the play needed no such adaptation: "in the old Indian plays the god comes forth and re-enacts his incarnations."

When Miller began writing this play he did not have in mind that Maggie would die, but rather that she and Quentin would part. But as the role developed "she seemed more inescapably fated." Her death also separated her in Miller's mind from Marilyn, "who as far as I knew was busy making films again, had bought herself a house, and was probably leading as good a working life as the movie business would permit." The

Barbara Loden as Maggie and Jason Robards as Quentin in the 1964 production
of *After the Fall* at the ANTA Washington Square Theatre in New York

Josette Simon as Maggie and Alibe Parsons as Carrie in the 1990 production
of *After the Fall* at the National Theatre in London

news of her death came to him while he was thinking about the last act of *After the Fall*. Arthur Jacobs, Monroe's public relations representative in New York, telephoned Miller in Connecticut on August 5, 1962 to deliver the news. "It's your problem," Miller responded abruptly, "not mine."

The playwright did not attend her funeral at the Westwood Village Memorial Chapel in Los Angeles, though his father went in his place. Izzy Miller remembered Marilyn's kindness when she asked him to escort her to Madison Square Garden a few months before, where she introduced him to John F. Kennedy after her steamy rendition of "Happy Birthday, Mr. President." What a story! In 2003—the same year Kermit Miller died, aged 91, on his brother's 88th birthday, October 17—Miller began work on a new play about a sultry movie star called *Finishing the Picture*.

In the 1960s Miller became increasingly involved with the volatile political climate in America. As protests on college campuses escalated against the war in Vietnam, his tall, Lincolnesque presence made him conspicuous as the closest thing the country had to a publicly engaged intellectual. To the Left he became something of a folk-hero, the moral spokesperson who stood up to McCarthyism when it took "guts" to do so. At a huge demonstration in New Haven, Connecticut he appeared with a fellow activist, the Rev. William Sloan Coffin, Jr.; and in 1965 he returned to the University of Michigan, where his daughter Jane was now a student, to participate in a well-publicized teach-in that closed down classes in Ann Arbor for three days, part of the nationwide college protests against the war in Southeast Asia. That same year Miller was elected President of PEN, the international literary organization of poets, essayists and novelists, known for its stand against censorship in all forms in its battle for the basic human right of freedom of expression. In 1968, with the Vietnam War still raging, and with the deaths of Robert Kennedy and Martin Luther King only months before, the playwright served as a delegate from Connecticut to the Democratic National Convention. There were riots in the streets of Chicago.

Miller and Yale chaplain William Sloan Coffin, Jr. leading a peace march in New Haven, Connecticut, March 1968

Miller's collection of short stories, *I Don't Need You Anymore*, was published by Viking Press in the midst of national turmoil. The nine works included in this 1967 collection are surprisingly intimate, though Miller later said that there was something "personal" about everything he wrote. The title story is a coming-of-age tale in which a young Jewish boy, alone on a windy Rockaway beach on the festival of "Tisha-bov or Rosh Hashanah or Yom Kippur," experiences something of a secular revelation that brings him closer to his own sense of separateness and self-identity. A stylized dramatization of this narrative was included in the documentary "Arthur Miller on Home Ground," which Harry Rasky directed for Canadian television in 1979.

A year after *I Don't Need You Anymore* appeared, *The Price* opened on Broadway. This four-character ensemble piece that Miller wrote in 1967 is unapologetic about being haunted by the past. On a superficial level *The Price* retraces familiar territory: a conflict between two brothers, their incomplete relationship with the controlling figure of their father and a wife who tries to anchor their actions in something resembling everyday reality. Miller adds the ambiguous figure of Gregory Solomon to the mix, the 89-year-old used-furniture dealer who is both delight-ed and overwhelmed by the prospect of buying the family heirlooms and starting "business" all over again. When the play opened at the Morosco Theatre on February 7, 1968, the same year in which the *Death of a Salesman* playscript sold its millionth copy, it was treated as "something that had dropped out of a car." But "behind a play about two brothers in conflict," the playwright said, "lay two forces: the Vietnam War and the theater of the absurd."

Miller's uneasiness with the absurdist tradition was based on his sense that it had mistaken irony for tragedy. Though in later years he would greatly admire Simon McBurney's rendition of Ionesco's *The Chairs* for Complicite when he saw it performed on Broadway, in the 1960s he was still very much attached to the idea that a persuasive drama had to be "a totally articulated work instead of an anecdote." Miller remained equally unsympathetic to experimental theater: he said,

Harold Gary as Gregory Solomon, Pat Hingle as Victor Franz, Kate Reid as Esther Franz and Arthur Kennedy as Walter Franz in the 1969 Broadway production of *The Price*

for example, that the Wooster Group was after "a minimalist conceit" when he took legal action in 1984 to block Elizabeth LeCompte's appropriation of scenes from *The Crucible* into her own adventurous work. He called *The Price*, by contrast, a "quartet," "the most specific play I've ever written." His dramatic language, he said, was "composed," "not dialogue caught through a key hole." However much the play-wright's comments reveal a misunderstanding of other dramatic styles, they nevertheless display a sensibility "rather like the [play's] table that occupies center stage." According to Michael Billington, this is one that "has a mahogany durability that resists the passage of time."

Directors have had a hard time unearthing the political subtext Miller said he built into this play. Written at a time of collective "amnesia"—the American war in Southeast Asia displayed a tragic disregard for and a painful repetition of European colonial misadventure—*The Price* depends for its momentum on a series of dramatic revelations. All of them document the price each character pays for distorting and forgetting the power of the past. As David Richards wrote in 1992, reviewing John Tillinger's New York revival starring Hector Elizondo, Joe Spano and Eli Wallach for the Roundabout Theatre Company, "one way or another, the bills will be paid. The piper never gets stiffed."

Set in Manhattan in mid-afternoon on a Saturday in winter, 1966, *The Price* takes place in real time. The interval separating the two scenes is merely a break in the play's continuous action. As the second act begins, Walter Franz, the successful surgeon who arrives near the end of the first act to meet his brother Victor in the West Side attic where the family furniture is stored, has still not taken off his expensive overcoat. Sixteen years have passed since their last encounter. "The father is dead," the playwright observed. (His own father, Isidore Miller, died in 1966 at the age of 81 in a Long Island nursing home.) "The sons have to deal with their own characters." Everything from the past, an armoire, a cabinet, a crystal radio, a library table, a wind-up record player, a fencing foil, a single oar and a harp, must be itemized, tagged and sold. "The more you can throw away the more it's beautiful," intones the assessor, Gregory Solomon. But the one thing these brothers cannot throw away, try as they might, is their shared past.

On Miller's set that past is made palpable, haunting and real. Props anchor the play and serve to advance a compelling story in which family secrets turn out not to have been secrets after all. "With furniture like this," says the well-named Solomon, who now occupies the father's overstuffed chair, "the shopping is over." Boris Aronson, who designed the set for the play's premiere, said that on this stage the "furniture was more than real." The characters' decisions were made years before, during the same fateful decade that followed the Crash of 1929; the Depression, whose discarded emblems lie piled up before us on stage making their last stand, determined their lives and ended the only security, however frail, these brothers will ever have. "We invent ourselves, Vic, to wipe out what we know." Walter chose to make a new life for himself: Victor stayed behind. But in both cases, as the playwright observed, "They'll never rid themselves of their father."

The intimate scale of *The Price*, a carefully shaped work, has proven to be the source of its greatest appeal. Actors continue to be attracted to the wide emotional range built into the four roles Miller has written for them, as well as to the text's demands for strong ensemble playing. In this fraternal confrontation all arguments are evenly balanced; it all "depends on your point of view." The play's image "began with the laugh record"; the finished work had its origins in an unmanageable television script called *It Is You, Victor*, as well as in discarded material from *After the Fall*, especially in the early pages of a draft known as *The Third Play*. Pat Hingle and Kate Reid were in the original cast; the set included a large mahogany table that had actually belonged to the playwright's parents and was still being used by his aunt. The show ran for 426 performances though, according to Miller, Ulu Grosbard's production "wasn't synchronized" (most critics agreed). During rehearsals, the playwright took over the direction himself. Fielder Cook's Emmy Award-winning television version for the "Hallmark Hall of Fame" in 1971, with George C. Scott as Victor Franz, was more sharply articulated and evenly paced. After a run at the small Harold Clurman Theater on the stretch of West 42nd Street known as Theater Row, *The Price* returned to Broadway in 1979 starring Fritz Weaver, Mitchell Ryan and Joseph Buloff. John Stix's interpretation had previously won accolades when it was shown at the Spoleto Festival USA in Charleston, South Carolina. Twenty years later James Naughton directed Harris Yulin, Jeffrey DeMunn and Bob Dishy in the principal roles for the Williamstown Theatre Festival in a production that later

George C. Scott as Victor Franz, Colleen Dewhurst as Esther Franz and Barry Sullivan
as Walter Franz in the television version of *The Price*, 1971

transferred to the Royale Theatre on West 45th Street. And in 2003 the
veteran Miller actor Warren Mitchell played Gregory Solomon in
London's West End, where Sean Holmes's production lost little of the
fierce ensemble drive it had had as originally mounted on a more
modest scale at the Tricycle Theatre. Reflecting on his belated success
with this vastly underrated work, the playwright mused, "The time is
now right for *The Price*."

Miller said he based the character of Gregory Solomon on an old
furniture salesman he had met years before, when a friend needed his

services. "His Russian–Yiddish inflections still have the power to make me laugh." (The playwright may also have based Solomon's speech patterns on "Boris Aronson talk"; the designer's accent was as celebrated as his sets all over Broadway.) The play's Solomon, however, is a far cry from a comic figure; his ironic laughter is heavily mediated by recollections of suicide, divorce, mental illness and the failure of personal ambition. His endurance is what counted most for the playwright. Actors have struggled to find the modulation Miller built into this complex role: play the part for laughs and the work falls apart.

Comedy was a genre that in any case did not come easily to Miller. His attempts to write in this vein generally met with decidedly mixed results. In 1970 he composed for television what he called a "shortish play," *Fame*, about a Neil Simon–like playwright "in his 30's and how he copes with the unexpected ramifications of sudden success." It was not broadcast on NBC until eight years later. Starring a handsome Richard Benjamin in the lead role, the script's intended humor nonetheless fell flat on the television screen. *The Creation of the World and Other Business*, imagined as a tongue-in-cheek retelling of the Book of Genesis, opened at the Schubert Theatre in New York on November 30, 1972, but closed after twenty performances. Barbara Harris left the show during tryouts in Washington, D.C., as did the director Harold Clurman. The play was greeted by devastating reviews on Broadway, even with Zoe Caldwell and Bob Dishy as the accomplished headliners.

Miller's musical version of the same play, *Up from Paradise*, with music by Stanley Silverman, was staged two years later at the Power Center for the Performing Arts at the University of Michigan in Ann Arbor, where it ran for a scheduled five days. The design team included

THE UNIVERSITY OF MICHIGAN THEATRE PROGRAMS

# UP FROM PARADISE

April 23-28, 1974
The Power Center for the Performing Arts

Program cover of *Up from Paradise*, April 1974, featuring a caricature of Miller by Al Hirschfeld

faculty members Zelma Weisfeld, Alan Billings and R. Craig Wolf. Miller read the narration himself and the program cover featured a caricature of the author by Al Hirschfeld. With "lots of rewrites," what Miller called his "heavenly cabaret" resurfaced in 1983 at the 100-seat Jewish Repertory Theater on 14th Street in Manhattan. Ran Avni's production featured Len Cariou as God, Austin Pendleton and Alice Playten as Adam and Eve, and Lonny Price as Abel. Even with so many talents "pulling for Arthur," the "entertainment" still had problems finding an audience.

The playwright found a more congenial idiom, and a decidedly political one, with the writing of *The Archbishop's Ceiling* in 1975. Though the producers chose to close the play in Washington, D.C. after disappointing tryouts at the Kennedy Center, where the work opened in 1977 with Bibi Andersson and John Cullum under Arvin Brown's direction, the revised version for the Bristol Old Vic (1985) and the Royal Shakespeare Company at the Barbican Pit (1986) marked the beginning of what was to become the enthusiastic revival and reception of Miller's work in England. As the director David Thacker later remarked, "In the U.K. we consider him only a little lower than Shakespeare but a little higher than God."

*The Archbishop's Ceiling* reflects Miller's long association with PEN, especially during the years he served as joint vice president with Harold Pinter. Together they monitored not only the censorship of artists in Eastern Europe, but also political abuse in Turkey, where the two playwrights traveled on behalf of the human rights organization. Miller sets his play in a capital city of an unidentified Eastern bloc country, though he later acknowledged that he was thinking about Czechoslovakia. Like Tom Stoppard's *Professional Foul* and David Edgar's *Pentecost*, the piece measures the price the life of the mind is forced to pay as a consequence of the lethal East-West divide. Adrian, a privileged American writer nurtured by ideals of freedom of expression—but provincial and naïve nonetheless—arrives at the former palace of an archbishop, where he encounters the dissident writer Sigmund, a figure Miller modeled on

Miller with fellow PEN member, Harold Pinter, Istanbul, 1986

his fellow playwright Vaclav Havel. The action takes place in the archbishop's sitting room under a frescoed ceiling, which may or may not
be bugged. Miller described the listening device as something "like
God. You never know whether he's there or not but you have to take
account of him anyway." He said he wanted to dramatize "what happens…when people know they are…at all times talking to Power,
whether through a bug or a friend who is really an informer." Under
such circumstances one becomes "fascinated with reality"—"whether
or not there is any."

Adrian, the novelist who admits to liking "ambiguity," "providing it's
clear," will never understand the politics configured, then swiftly recon-
figured, under this archbishop's painted ceiling, where God has become
"simply a form of art." On this set, a challenge for any designer, the
ground constantly shifts; for the play's characters, "impersonators" really, are "always making theatre." "It's everywhere that people pretend,"
even on that supposedly "safe" space, off-center and "off-mike," to
which the mercurial Maya repairs to speak something like—but probably not—"the truth." By 1990 the politics in the play had come full
circle: Vaclav Havel, by now the Czech president, invited Miller to
Prague for a production of *The Archbishop's Ceiling*. A year later the play
had its much delayed New York premiere at Lincoln Center.

In 1980 Joan Copeland was cast in the role of Rose Baum in a new
Miller play slated to appear on Broadway that November. The part was
based on the figure of their mother Gussie, and the play, *The American
Clock*, "a kind of vaudeville" inspired by Studs Terkel's *Hard Times: An
Oral History of the Great Depression in America*, was intended to be both
autobiographical and epic. (The playwright's daughter Rebecca was in
the cast when the television version was broadcast on TNT in 1993.) At
the Spoleto Festival in Charleston a few months earlier, the "grand
movement" of *The American Clock* received enthusiastic notices, but by
the time Daniel Sullivan's production opened at the Biltmore Theatre in
New York it had lost much of its original spark; it closed after twelve

The 1985 production of *The Archbishop's Ceiling* at the Old Vic

Miller's sister Joan Copeland as Rose Baum and John Randolph as Moe Baum
in the 1980 Broadway production of *The American Clock*

performances. Miller reworked the script in 1984 for Peter Wood's
dynamic production in London, where it was a notable success when it
opened two years later at the National. After playing in the intimate
Cottesloe, it was later reblocked for the wider proscenium space of the
Lyttleton. Miller's revisions have been incorporated into the standard
text for the play, as used by Austin Pendleton in 1988 for the
Williamstown Theatre Festival and for the New York revival by the
Signature Theatre Company in 1997.

The work's fluid structure, "a picture of people interacting with
each other and with a significant historical event," demanded a strong
stage solution. Peter Wood took his cue from the popular music of the
Depression years which, as the playwright said, was "all happy" in tunes
like "I Can't Give You Anything But Love" and "Sunny Side of the

Miller's daughter Rebecca as Edie, with Loren Dean, in the 1993 television version of *The American Clock*

Street." Relying on his talented cast, including Sara Kestleman and Michael Bryant in the roles that pay homage to Miller's parents, the director made the enclosed family circle the focal point for under-standing the work's larger political setting. "It was all happening right there," the playwright said, "in the living room." Short scenes of "hard times" from all over America (where, as Harry Hopkins observed, "hunger" was "not debatable") play in sharp counterpoint to the Baums' closely observed slide down the '30s economic ladder. An exec-utive from General Motors now manages a bowling alley in Toledo, Ohio; Rose Baum pawns her jewelry and sells her piano, her last link to Gershwin, certainty and sanity—all to the background music of popular tunes. Lee Baum, the Miller figure (played by look-alike Neil Daglish in Wood's production) dreams of a university education, but he, too, loses his prized possession, the same Columbia Racer bicycle the playwright remembered from his own youth. "My idea was not to be chained to the continuity as in a realistic work," Miller wrote in a letter to Peter Wood. The "presentational" style of *The American Clock* created, instead, "a mural," "a mosaic" tracing the Depression's most pernicious legacy, the loss of possibility and the loss of hope: "It's a story of America talking to itself." He added: "There's never been a society that hasn't had a clock running on it, and you can't help wondering— How long?"

In 1980 Miller was also thinking about another form of doom, this one equally informed by documentation and historical memory. He had spent a month the previous year working on a commission for a television adaptation of *The Musicians of Auschwitz*, Fania Fenelon's compelling memoir written with Marcelle Routier. "I tried to treat it as a story meaningful to the survivors, by which I mean all of us," Miller said. "I didn't want it to be a mere horror story." Fenelon, whose father was Jewish, was a popular cabaret singer in Paris; when she was arrested in the systematic roundup of Jews by the French police and deported to a concentration camp, she proudly called out her real name, which was Goldstein. "If I was going to die," she wrote, "I preferred to die under my father's name." During the dehumanizing train journey to the camps she befriended another half-Jewish girl, Marianne, and it is Fenelon's vivid memory that bears witness to the moral complexity of relationships in an all-female world consigned to an ignominious fate. At Auschwitz-Birkenau, she discovers, music-lovers, including the infamous Dr. Mengele, are also barbarians.

Miller said that what attracted him to Fenelon's story was the uncompromising way it showed how "it was possible to exercise free will even in a concentration camp." The situation she described "was emblematic for Jews and for the human race; it revealed mankind at the abyss." What Fenelon says in a key speech in Miller's play is central to his scenario: "We know a little something about the human race that we didn't know before. And it's not good news." Fenelon survived, while 12,000 others perished each day, only because she played in a band whose interludes accompanied a steady march to the gas chambers. Nazi perversity also encouraged the half-starved, all-woman orchestra to concentrate on the German classics.

In his television script, *Playing for Time*, Miller's through-line relies on his success in transforming Fenelon's demoralized fellow inmates into the multidimensionality of believable dramatic personalities. His strongest portraits can be found in the evocative psychological detail he locates in the women themselves, not in male protagonists like the demonic Mengele, the absurdly "sensitive" German officer or even in the mysterious Shmuel, who despite his prophecies still plays a satellite role. Fenelon's diminished expectations of herself and of the women around her are traced in a series of heartrending interactions devoid of all sentimentality: with Alma, the strict and correct kapo-conductor who defines herself as an artist and a Germanist but who is unwittingly poisoned without ever understanding that she dies only because she is one more "dirty" Jew; with the Polish women who are allowed to keep their hair and fail to recognize that the Jewish victims are merely pale reflections of themselves; with the female guard who "saves" a child from the arms of his distraught mother on her way to being gassed, then abandons her Jewish "pet" when requested to do so for the "good" of the Fatherland; and finally with Marianne herself, who sells her body to the nearest Nazi soldier for a piece of sausage. Fania asks Marianne how she will be able to live with herself if she survives; yet she is forced to confront the depths of her own ugliness when she shares in her friend's booty. An extra crust of bread brings both nourishment and despair. Women no longer menstruate; younger ones forge exclusive romantic alliances with one another. Tribalism is even more pernicious in eroding any sense of purposeful identity. "I am sick of the Zionists-and-the-Marxists; the Jews-and-the-Gentiles; the Easterners-and-the-Westerners; the Germans-and-the-non-Germans; the French-and-the-non-French," Miller's Fania, the half-Jew-half-Gentile, proclaims in a moment of painful lucidity. "I am sick of it, sick of it, sick of it! I am a woman, not a tribe! And I am humiliated! That is all I know."

Filmed in November 1979 in an abandoned army base in Fort Indiantown Gap, Pennsylvania, which had been used to detain German prisoners of war, *Playing for Time* was broadcast on CBS on September 30, 1980. The date coincided with the first night of Rosh Hashanah, the Jewish New Year. Daniel Mann's searing production was hailed by John J. O'Connor in the *New York Times* as "totally uncompromising" and "heartbreakingly poignant." The two-and-a-half-hour play was shown without commercial interruption, but only because advertisers refused to buy time for a project that was at the center of a bruising critical storm. Vanessa Redgrave, well-known for her ardent support of the Palestinian cause, had been cast in the lead, a part for which Jane Fonda and Barbra Streisand had previously been considered. During her acceptance speech for the Academy Award as Best Supporting Actress for her work in the title role in *Julia*, the film based on Lillian Hellman's story, Redgrave had been booed off the stage when she denounced as "Zionist hoodlums" those protestors who had traveled to Los Angeles to embarrass her by calling her politics into question. Even Fenelon had been brought into the fray, saying at one point that "she can't play me." Miller, who knew something about blacklisting at first hand, stood by the casting choice, at one point claiming that he was even unaware of Redgrave's "activist" stance. He said the actress was chosen for her talent, not her beliefs. Critics seemed to agree.

Vanessa Redgrave, who shaved her head for the part, then literally starved herself and scratched scars onto her scalp and face, received an Emmy Award for her haunting portrayal of Fania Fenelon. She shared top honors with Jane Alexander, who played Alma Rose (Gustav Mahler's niece), as well as with the playwright, whose teleplay was also cited with an Outstanding Drama Special Award. Miller's stage version of this powerful play, completed five years later, was treated as a significant event at the Edinburgh International Festival in 1986. It has yet to receive a major production in London or New York.

Vanessa Redgrave (left) in *Playing for Time*, 1980, scripted for television by Miller

Miller's principal project of the 1980s was the publication of his autobiography *Timebends*. As he approached his seventieth year, he characterized the volume as "a preemptive strike" against a dozen or so would-be chroniclers anxious to tell his story. In turn both intimate and oddly distant, the writing, often eloquent, attempts to structure time "as the mind does," synchronizing memory through a highly selective process of free association. Omitting many details while dramatizing several others at the expense of "mere fact," *Timebends* skillfully manipulates subjectivity as it simultaneously reveals and conceals. This is no doubt part of the book's fascination. It was also part of the negative reception the autobiography received in some quarters (almost exclusively in the writer's own country) when it appeared in 1987. "The kiss without the tell," he wrote, especially in regard to what he chose *not* to say about his famous involvement with Marilyn Monroe, "simply doesn't register as interesting, let alone honest."

Four of the new Miller works staged in the same decade display a similar fascination with "the colors of memory." *Elegy for a Lady*, a play about retrospective regret, opened at the Long Wharf Theatre in New Haven, Connecticut on October 26, 1982, directed by the author himself. Rich in subtext and based on a short story published in *Esquire*, this brief two-hander measures the shifting ground beneath an accidental

Miller on the set of *Elegy for a Lady* at the Long Wharf Theatre, New Haven, Connecticut, 1982

encounter. As a man enters a shop in search of an appropriate gift for the lover he says is "dying," he forges an uneasy alliance with a female figure, "filled with love and anguish," identified only as the Proprietress. The dialogue is cryptic, in places even elliptical, and shows the playwright at his most Pinteresque. *Some Kind of Love Story* appeared on the same bill, originally called *2 by A.M.* but later changed to *Two-Way Mirror.* The second play has a completely different tempo: the fast-paced dialogue between a detective and a former call girl aims to crack a case that remains unsolved after five years. Memory is in this instance alternately unreliable and perverse, for the key witness, Angela, is "delusionary." David Thacker's 1989 London production of the twin bill for the Young Vic, starring Helen Mirren and Bob Peck, was warmly received, though the American premiere with Christine Lahti was savaged by the critics.

The recuperation of a verifiable past is also at stake in a second double-bill from the same period, *Danger: Memory!* Gregory Mosher's production of *I Can't Remember Anything* and *Clara* opened at the Mitzi E. Newhouse Theater at Lincoln Center in New York on February 8, 1987. In the first play Geraldine Fitzgerald was cast in the role of Leonora, a reclusive New England widow who *won't* remember anything; she retreats into Scotch rather than confront the unfulfilled promise of her youth. Her husband's best friend Leo, an unregenerate progressive whose ideals were formed in the Depression, gently coaxes her to reassemble the fragments of their shared history. She resists, suggesting a bumpy samba instead. Always an uncomfortable road to travel, the past, Leo reminds us, was also joyous in its hope for mankind. Though never dramatically articulated, something more than personal nostalgia lurks in the political background of the play: how lives are shattered when a world turns its back on long-held assumptions and ingrained beliefs about social responsibility. When Joan Copeland and Eli Wallach did a reading of the play on February 28, 2005 at the National Arts Club in New York as part of "A Tribute to Arthur Miller," it became clear that *I Can't Remember Anything* was also about fear, loneliness and denial, as well as the need for human connection, especially in old age. Leonora, the intrusive widow-next-door (in this case, down the road), cries out for one last attachment; Leo, true to himself, retreats into separateness and solitude.

The companion piece, *Clara*, features a weary police veteran ready to "do what they all do: sit looking at the ocean somewhere, wondering where my life went." Searching for clues to the murder of the 28-year-old social worker who gives her name to the play, he directs his questions to her grief-stricken father, Albert Kroll. The detective story suddenly changes direction when the play turns inward. As Kroll slowly recalls incidents from the past that may or may not have something to do with Clara's death, he is forced to examine the liberal ideals that helped shape her young life. He soon suspects that one of her "rehabilitated" clients, a Puerto Rican who served time for killing his girlfriend, may have murdered again. Kenneth MacMillan's sturdy performance in the original production traced Kroll's increasing horror as he slowly comes to recognize the former convict as his daughter's demon-lover. Now he must confront not only despair, but also the ugly racism he has long sought to suppress. Detective Lieutenant Fine gives voice to Kroll's worst feelings about himself when he declares that he believes in only "greed and race: blacks for blacks, whites for whites, Jews for Jews." In 1991 Darren McGavin and William Daniels took the lead roles when this unsettling play about the danger of memory was adapted for television on the Arts & Entertainment Network.

A year after the American premiere of *Danger: Memory!* Miller completed a film script originally entitled *Almost Everybody Wins*. This story deals with deception, individual and collective, and on a superficial level resembles the situation dramatized in *Some Kind of Love Story*. In the scenario a hot-shot private investigator, the lapsed Catholic Tom O'Toole, has been summoned to a decaying New England mill town, the fictional Highbury, on the suspicion that the teenage boy convicted of murdering the local doctor has been wrongly incarcerated for the crime. Angela, "a one-woman political and sexual scandal," tries to hold

Debra Winger and Frank Military in the 1990 film *Everybody Wins*, scripted by Miller and directed by Karel Reisz

on to whatever reality she can as O'Toole tries to piece together the ever-elusive truth. In 1973 the playwright had been a moving force behind the real-life case of Peter Reilly, the 18-year-old who, his friends and neighbors in Connecticut were convinced, had been falsely convicted of manslaughter in the brutal killing of his mother. After Miller brought in his own lawyer and alerted the *New York Times* to the story, all charges were dismissed in a new trial three years later when it was revealed that the prosecutor had concealed evidence proving that Reilly had been miles away from the scene when the murder was committed. Miller's film script goes much further in developing the undercurrents of corruption "everyone" seems so desperate to conceal. In *Everybody Wins*, the title by which the film directed by Karel Reisz was released in 1990 starring Debra Winger and Nick Nolte, the town doctor is the kingpin in the local drug trade, which also involves elected city officials, the police and several other characters holding less reputable positions; everyone knows who committed the crime; and all the key players are implicated in the cover-up. Only the mercurial Angela speaks against the travesty of justice, albeit ambiguously. In this cynical tale of lust and revenge, murder, conspiracy and seduction, "what seems," as the director said, "is not always what is." "It's about reality and the arbitrary way we do decide it's real," Miller suggested. "Through the evolution of the story—a murder that took place before the story opens—we will be put through an exercise in experiencing reality and unreality." Shot in Norwich, Connecticut and in studios in Wilmington, North Carolina, *Everybody Wins*, which suffered from several editing problems, including lapses in continuity, never achieved the potential built into the script. Its final frame, nonetheless, is particularly unnerving and implies what this project might have become. Underlining Miller's central motif, the town's collaborators gather on a frosty lawn for a conciliatory cocktail party, reaffirming their status in a retooled balance of power. Everybody knows everybody's guilty: "This way everybody wins."

In the 1990s Miller worked on five plays that kept him busy well through the turn of the century. *The Ride Down Mt. Morgan*, which the playwright called "a completely political play" about greed and self-aggrandizement in the Reagan years, had its debut in London under Michael Blakemore's direction in 1991, starring Tom Conti, Gemma Jones and Clare Higgins. Although the playwright found "the atmosphere" in England "friendlier," the production never succeeded in reconciling the script's multiple perspectives of fantasy, flashback and temporal reality. "The play is really a kind of nightmare," he said. "It ought to flow rapidly and effortlessly from one moment to another." He revised the text for Scott Elliott when he staged *Mt. Morgan* at the Williamstown Theatre Festival five years later, with F. Murray Abraham in the lead. The work achieved something like its final form in 1998 when, directed by David Esbjornson, Patrick Stewart's high-profile interpretation of George Lyman opened for a limited run in New York at the Public Theater and was restaged for Broadway two years later.

Miller's third version of *The Ride Down Mt. Morgan*, "a moral farce," attempts to shift the tone of the play. His male-menopausal anti-hero,

Clare Higgins and Tom Conti in the 1991 production of *The Ride Down Mt. Morgan*
at Wyndham's Theatre in London

too much of "a reptilian whiner" in earlier renditions, is now reimagined not only as some outrageous, egomaniacal life force, but also as an embodiment of unbridled passion, whose every action shows him "running away from death every single day of his life." His worst fears come back to haunt him when he crashes his Porsche on a snowy mountain and breaks every bone in his body. We see the consequences of the two marriages he has conducted simultaneously for the past nine years when two wives confront each other for the first time—as do two children—at his hospital bedside. In what is essentially Lyman's play, fantasy always vies with reality, but others pay the price for both.

Miller's female characters come in for additional strain in his next play, *The Last Yankee*, which opened on January 21, 1993 in two cross-Atlantic productions: John Tillinger's at the Manhattan Theatre Club and David Thacker's at the Young Vic in London. An earlier, 20-minute version shown at the Ensemble Studio Theatre in New York portrayed two unlikely strangers who meet in the visitors' room of a state mental institution, where they wait to see wives who suffer from chronic depression. These husbands have been no great help in fighting it. Although in developing this project Miller brings their partners on stage—the dutiful one married to a talky businessman displays a long-suppressed liveliness by donning formal dancing attire and efficiently tapping her way through "Swanee"—the locus of offstage action is securely set in masculine hands. Leroy, whose Puritan self-reliance marks him as the last Yankee of the piece, is the "Hamilton" who finds fulfillment working as a carpenter but thwarts his wife's ambitions by moving their seven children and their distinguished name too many notches down the social and economic ladder. The entrepreneur John Frick is, by contrast, upwardly mobile, though in this case the state of marriage is rendered even more precarious. The role of his troubled wife Karen, however, especially as interpreted by Rose Gregorio in the American premiere and by Shami Chaikin for the Signature Theatre Company in 1998 (when *The Last Yankee* was directed by Joseph Chaikin on a double-bill with *I Can't Remember Anything* as part of a season devoted to Miller), provides one of the more enlivening possibilities for the staging of this play.

Some of the same tensions are evident in *Broken Glass*, Miller's most substantial work from this productive late period. "Full of ambiguities," the play is nonetheless far more secure in examining private neurosis within a framework of public concern and "the juncture where they actually meet." The scene is set in Brooklyn, 1938, though the "real" action, "the culmination of five years of assaults on the Jewish inhabitants of Germany," takes place miles away: Kristallnacht, the November night of broken glass when, in an organized pogrom, the Nazis torched and destroyed at least 7,500 shops, 11 synagogues, Jewish community centers and cemetery chapels, 29 warehouses and 171 homes. More than 30,000 Jewish men were rounded up and thrown into concentration

Rose Gregorio as Karen Frick and Tom Aldredge as John Frick in the 1993 production of *The Last Yankee* at the Manhattan Theatre Club, New York

camps. As Christopher Bigsby noted, "The world reacted with horror and little else."

Sylvia Gellburg, the drama's central female figure, is cauterized by a newspaper report that two old Jews have been forced, sadistically, to clean a sidewalk with nothing more than a toothbrush. "Where's Roosevelt?" she cries out in despair as she is suddenly struck down by a psychosomatic paralysis. "Where's England?"

Miller complicates the narrative by offering us clues to character based on dialogue rather than stage action. As David Richards observed when the play opened at the Booth Theatre in New York on April 24, 1994, "Sylvia Gellburg is unable to walk because her husband is a cripple." Hers is a marriage that failed. Miller tightens the knot: Phillip Gellburg, "the only Jew who ever worked for Brooklyn Guarantee in their whole history," has been living an assimilationist's nightmare. Proud of the fact that he pushed his son, "the only Jewish captain in the Army," to attend West Point, Gellburg—"not Goldberg," as he reminds us—painfully confuses access with acceptance. He remains confounded by his wife's sudden illness, wondering if "getting this hysterical about something on the other side of the world is sane." What he fails to see is that the dire events taking place in Germany are only a grotesque extension of what is happening right "around the corner"—fails to see it, that is, until his establishment boss, the country-club anti-Semite Stanton Case (always happy to use "the Jew" to do the bank's dirty work), accuses him of collusion with another "of his own kind." The world this "correct" but self-hating Jew has so tightly constructed for himself, which includes, significantly, his secret twenty-year sexual impotence, is about to come crashing down all around him.

*Broken Glass* includes one additional Jewish character whose importance in the Broadway production, and to the play as a whole, may have been undermined by a late cast change that replaced Ron Silver with David Dukes in the role of Dr. Harry Hyman. An unregenerate as well as an unreflective Freudian, this attractive and charismatic figure, played with unusual restraint by Mandy Patinkin in London, is married to a

Margot Leicester and Henry Goodman in the 1994 production of *Broken Glass* at the National Theatre in London, later televised and broadcast on PBS in 1996

Gentile and wears expensive leather boots when he goes horseback riding on Ocean Parkway. In ways that Miller may not have intended, the most spirited and most psychologically stable characters in *Broken Glass* seem to be those who most defy identifiable Jewish stereotypes. Or perhaps Miller is inadvertently playing with other stereotypes here: Harry is, after all, that familiar, highly accomplished Jewish male—a doctor, no less—who forms an alliance with a specifically non-Jewish, i.e., non-neurotic, wife. The only complication is that Miller's doctor falls in love with the emotionally starved Sylvia. "What did I do with my life?" she wonders with pitch-perfect lucidity in what is, perhaps, the play's most arresting moment. "I took better care of my shoes."

Amy Irving and Ron Rifkin took the leads in John Tillinger's premiere, though an elaborate revolve on the busy set designed by Santo Loquasto may have inhibited the intimate scale of the actors' ten economical scenes. Miller changed the ending of the play for New York: in the pre-Broadway run at the Long Wharf Theatre it was not clear that Sylvia's realization that "she has been tiptoeing around her life for 30 years" comes at the expense of her husband's death. David Thacker's crisp London staging of this Olivier Award-winning Best Play later that same year seemed more attuned to the atmosphere of foreboding and unrelenting anguish, and also more nuanced in its exploration of human passivity in the face of looming disaster. Margot Leicester and Henry Goodman repeated their highly praised performances when Thacker adapted his National Theatre production for BBC television, which was broadcast in the United States on October 18, 1996 as a "Masterpiece Theater" presentation for PBS. The veteran director of several major Miller revivals in England is also credited with giving the author the final title for his play: earlier incarnations were entitled *The Man in Black* and, simply, *Gellburg*.

Miller said that decades before he wrote *Broken Glass* he did indeed know a woman who, like the Sylvia in his play, suffered "hysterical paralysis" from the waist down; her husband dressed only in black. "It was only a few years ago," he said in 1996, "that the husband's connection leaped out at me." And yet the real paralysis that informs the background of this work is the one "that could destroy the world." Miller aims to take "us back to the time when the social contract was being torn up," when the road of indifference led to complicity, when, as Sylvia says, all the "streets are covered with broken glass." In this play, his thirteenth to open on Broadway, Miller's conflation of personal doom and historical atrocity may be shaky and flawed, yet its controlling metaphor of moral urgency continued his commitment to using stage reality for provocation and serious thought.

*Mr. Peters' Connections*, the eighty-minute piece that opened in New York on May 17, 1998 for a five weeks' run as part of the Signature

Peter Falk in *Mr. Peters' Connections* in the Signature Theatre production, New York, 1998

Theatre's Miller season, found the playwright in a very different mood, one that returned him to territory previously explored in *The Ride Down Mt. Morgan*. If, in the case of George Lyman, Miller presented us with the convincing portrait of a priapic male who not only dreams but lives his fantasy, here a similar narcissism seems to have aged badly and slowly gone to seed. Set in an abandoned Manhattan nightclub, this is a play with characters "both living and dead." What we are meant to see on stage "should look like whatever the reader or producer imagines as a space where the living and the dead may meet, the gray or blue or blazing red terrain of the sleeping mind where imagination runs free." Harry Peters, the ex-Pan Am pilot who is also an ex-Princeton instructor, is discovered alone on stage as he moves discontinuously from real memory to conjecture in an attempt to find "the subject," but what is in fact the meaning that will make his life cohere. The challenge for Garry Hynes, the Irish artistic director of the Druid Theatre Company in Galway, who traveled to New York to stage this production, was to organize this free-form line of thought in the absence of internal tension. The characters that appear in Harry's world are no more and no less substantial than images; we never see them from within. What we witness instead is the variable nature of aged memory: "I am older than everyone I ever knew." Miller's homage to Beckett, if in fact it is that, is limited to the onstage presence of a new pair of shoes, the prop that sets in motion a dreamlike state of suspended consciousness combining elements of comedy, fantasia and half-forgotten memory.

Such nonlinear thought includes allusions to Miller's earlier writings as well as to his own life, which run the gamut from the successful older brother who appears in *Death of a Salesman* to the enigmatic figure of Cathy-May, the object-like figure of desire who is an obvious stand-in for Norma Jean (Marilyn Monroe). The case for Miller as a writer of sympathetic parts for women is hardly advanced by this plot, for in Harry's case the sexism on display runs deep. In New York Anne Jackson made the most of the scenes in which she appeared as Harry's wife, but it was clear from the outset that the evening belonged to Peter Falk, the star of television's *Columbo*, in the title role. "I asked Arthur Miller how come he thought of me," the actor recalled. "He said he didn't know that many actors, so he asked his son-in-law Daniel Day-Lewis. And Daniel said, 'Well, you could give Peter Falk a call'." Another American actor, John Cullum, portrayed Harry Peters in Michael Blakemore's British premiere on July 20, 2000 at the Almeida Theatre, in a cast that included the seasoned London player Nicholas Woodeson. Giorgio Albertazzi, who replaced Mastroianni when he starred opposite Monica Vitti in the famous Zeffirelli *After the Fall*, was featured in *Il Mondo di Mr Peters*, Enrico Maria Lamanna's 2003 Italian production for Teatro di Roma in the skillful Masolino d'Amico translation.

In *Resurrection Blues* Miller could be seen moving his theater in still another direction, however problematic. David Esbjornson's ambitious production opened at the Guthrie Theater in Minneapolis on August 9,

Bruce Bohne as Stanley in the Guthrie Theater production of *Resurrection Blues*, 2002

2002; the East Coast premiere took place not in New York, but in Philadelphia. Under Jiri Zizka's direction for the Wilma Theatre Company, the play opened on September 24, 2003. A year later Mark Lamos staged a slightly revised version of the same piece in Los Angeles at the Mark Taper Forum.

According to the playwright, *Resurrection Blues* is "about advertising and media manipulation. It's about lying to the public." The scene is set in an unspecified South American country where, in the critic Toby Zinman's concise summary, "2% of the population owns 96% of the wealth, where drugs are the primary national product, guns are everywhere, and contaminated water destroys children's livers." As one of Miller's characters wryly comments, "After thirty-eight years of civil war, what did you expect to find here, Sweden?" The plot is set in motion when the local strongman plans to kill by crucifixion a strange young man who claims to be the son of God; an American television network offers $25 million for the rights to broadcast the execution. The satire, however, soon turns preachy, even as Miller's moral outrage yearns so ambitiously for its proper dramatic form.

In his 89th year, one more "fable of the perversion of the American dream" opened at the Goodman Theatre in Chicago. Robert Falls's production of *Finishing the Picture*, a play about a film director who must deal with an unstable starlet, opened in September 2004. "She's recognized all over the world, loved by millions, but unable to believe in herself," according to the Goodman's official summary. "The studio owners are threatening to pull the plug, and a temperamental acting teacher is flown in to coax the actress out of bed and onto the set." Even after the opening nights of more than two dozen professionally produced stage plays, and revivals of those works all over the world, the author was still trying to get his story right.

Asked what he wanted to be remembered for, Miller told Mel Gussow: "a few good parts for actors." Years before, recalling the thrill of playing stickball on an open lot overgrown with weeds in East Flatbush, when Brooklyn, despite the Depression, was so full of youthful promise, he still liked to think of himself as a "pretty good" second base-man—"not first," but "not third" either. Wearing his stature lightly as America's most enduring writer for the stage, Miller's self-assessment is, in the final analysis, as clear and honest as the work itself. "Up to a certain point the human being is completely unpredictable. That's what keeps me going," he said at the turn of the century. "You live long enough, you don't rust."

Arthur Miller died at his home in Roxbury, Connecticut on the evening of February 10, 2005, surrounded by close members of his family. Before returning to his farmhouse on Tophet Road he spent his last weeks being cared for at his sister's apartment on Central Park West. Only days before he died he told David Richenthal how much he was looking forward to the London production of *Death of a Salesman*, with Brian Dennehy reprising his role as Willy Loman. He promised to be there in May.

At the public memorial held in honor of Miller at the Majestic Theatre in New York on May 9, 2005, more than 1,500 people were in attendance. The crowd for admission crept down West 44th Street, wrapped around Schubert Alley and spilled over onto West 45th Street. Not everyone was able to get in. (When had that ever happened for an American dramatist before?) Miller, of course, had previously chosen the one word he wanted for his epitaph: "*writer.*"

# BIBLIOGRAPHY

BIGSBY, CHRISTOPHER. *A Critical Introduction to Twentieth-Century American Drama*, vol. 2. Cambridge: Cambridge University Press, 1984

—, ed. *Arthur Miller and Company*. London: Methuen, 1990

—, ed. *The Cambridge Companion to Arthur Miller*. Cambridge: Cambridge University Press, 1997

BRATER, ENOCH, ed. *Arthur Miller's America: Theater and Culture in a Time of Change.* Ann Arbor: University of Michigan Press, 2005

—, ed. *Global Miller.* Ann Arbor: University of Michigan Press, due 2006

CENTOLA, STEVE. *Arthur Miller in Conversation*. Dallas: Contemporary Research Associates, 1993

COHEN, SARAH B., ed. *From Hester Street to Hollywood: The Jewish-American Stage and Screen*. Bloomington: Indiana University Press, 1983

GOTTFRIED, MARTIN. *Arthur Miller: His Life and Work*. Cambridge, MA: Da Capo Press, 2003

GUSSOW, MEL. *Conversations with Miller*. New York: Applause Theatre & Cinema Books, 2002

KAZAN, ELIA. *Elia Kazan: A Life*. New York: Knopf, 1988

LEVIN, GAIL. "Making 'The Misfits'." Thirteen-WNET-New York, 2002

MARTIN, ROBERT A., ed. *Arthur Miller: New Perspectives*. Englewood Cliffs, NJ: Prentice-Hall, 1982

NAVASKY, VICTOR S. *Naming Names*. New York: Viking Press, 1980

RASKY, HARRY. "Arthur Miller on Home Ground." Canadian Broadcasting Company, 1979

ROUDANÉ, MATTHEW C., ed. *Conversations with Arthur Miller*. Jackson: University Press of Mississippi, 1987

ROWE, KENNETH T. *Write That Play!* New York: Funk and Wagnalls, 1939.

Arthur Miller in his writing studio in Roxbury, Connecticut, 1987.
Hanging on the wall is a large photograph of his parents

# ACKNOWLEDGMENTS

Much of what is included in this book is based on my many conversations with Arthur Miller, which began in the early 1980s and continued up until a few months before his death. Miller was a frequent visitor to Ann Arbor, and it was there, rather than in New York or at his home in Connecticut, that he seemed most open and relaxed in talking about his life and works. Inge Morath accompanied him on several of these occasions and was equally generous with her time. Often our conversations continued via telephone, and became especially pointed as the University of Michigan developed plans for the celebration of Miller's 85th year in October, 2000. I would also like to thank the playwright's son, Robert Miller, who traveled with his father to Ann Arbor in 1999, and Miller's sister, Joan Copeland, who has been throughout her busy career as an actress a gracious supporter of her brother's work. Anyone writing about Miller today owes an enormous debt, as I do, to Martin Gottfried, whose landmark biography first appeared in 2003; and also to Christopher Bigsby, who remains Miller's most conscientious and sympathetic critic. Harmon L. Remmel, Jean Ledwith King, E. Bryce Alpern and Giles G. Bole, Jr. have in their various ways been unusually kind and forthcoming in sharing their personal recollections about Ann Arbor during Miller's student years. Many other individuals have been just as helpful: Paul Unwin, who invited me to sit in on rehearsals of *The Man Who Had All the Luck* for its London premiere at the Young Vic; the BBC producer Louis Marks, who shared information with me about his television production of *The Crucible*; Darryl V. Jones, who directed a Dominican version of *A View from the Bridge*; the administrative officers of the Guthrie Theater in Minneapolis and the Lyric Opera in Chicago; the staff at the Principal's Office of Abraham Lincoln High School in Brooklyn; and the students who run the *Michigan Daily* and shared their ramshackle archives with me. The research departments at the Bentley Historical Library and the Special Collections Library at the University of Michigan have been unstinting in their efforts to help me locate the odd fact or missing piece of information. Kathryn L. Beam, for example, pointed me in the fruitful direction of the playwright's correspondence with Professor Kenneth Rowe, as well as to other material in the Miller files. The UM Video Services have been quick and efficient in responding to my queries, as have my colleagues at Michigan, Andrea Beauchamp, Laurence Goldstein, Inger Schultz, Zelma Weisfeld and William Bolcom. At Thames & Hudson I have been lucky to work with such fine professionals as Stanley Baron, Peter Warner, Samuel Clark, Katie Morgan and Jenny Wilson. Finally, I wish to express my gratitude to the Department of English Language and Literature, the LS&A Dean's Office and the Rackham School of Graduate Studies at the University of Michigan for their enthusiastic support of this project.

# SOURCES OF ILLUSTRATIONS

1. Photo © Elliott Erwitt/Magnum Photos; 5. Photo © Inge Morath/Magnum Photos; 6. Photo Arnold Newman/Getty Images; 8. Photo courtesy family album Inge Morath/Magnum Photos; 10. Courtesy Abraham Lincoln High School, Brooklyn; 12. Photo courtesy Bentley Historical Library, University of Michigan; 13. Photo courtesy Bentley Historical Library, University of Michigan; 15. Photo courtesy Bentley Historical Library, University of Michigan; 16 left. Photo courtesy Bentley Historical Library, University of Michigan; 16 right. Photo courtesy Bentley Historical Library, University of Michigan; 20 above. Photo courtesy Bentley Historical Library, University of Michigan; 20 below. Photo courtesy Bentley Historical Library, University of Michigan; 23 left. Photo courtesy Special Collections Library, University of Michigan; 23 right. Photo courtesy Special Collections Library, University of Michigan 24-25. Photo courtesy Bentley Historical Library, University of Michigan; 29. Photo © Dick Rose/Corbis; 30. Photo © Bettmann/Corbis; 33. Photo courtesy Ronald Grant Archive; 34. Courtesy Photofest; 35. Photo Eileen Darby/Getty Images; 40. Photo Robbie Jack/Corbis; 41. Photo courtesy Ronald Grant Archive; 42. Photo W. Eugene Smith/Getty Images; 43. Set design Jo Mielziner; 45. Photo Museum of the City of New York; 48. Photo © Inge Morath/Magnum Photos; 50. Photo © Inge Morath/Magnum Photos; 51. Photo Eric Y. Exit. Courtesy Goodman Theatre, Chicago; 52. Photo © Alfredo Valenta/Photofest; 54 left. Photo Museum of the City of New York; 54 right. Photo Museum of the City of New York; 56. Photo Hank Walker/Getty Images; 57. Printed by Benjamin Harris for Samuel Philips, Boston, 1693; 58. Photo © Inge Morath/Magnum Photos; 61. Photo courtesy Ronald Grant Archive; 64-65. Photo Joan Marcus; 69. Photo Paul Schutzer/Getty Images; 70. Courtesy Associated Press; 72. Photo Gordon Parks/Getty Images; 73. Photo Charles Hewitt/Getty Images; 77. Photo Inge Morath/Magnum; 78. Courtesy The National Theatre, London. Photo Nobby Clark; 81. Photo Dan Rest/Lyric Opera of Chicago; 84-85. Photo © 1961 United Artists. All Rights Reserved; 86. Photo Eve Arnold/Magnum Photos; 89. Photo Ian Berry/Magnum Photos; 90. Photo Inge Morath/Magnum Photos; 94. Photo Inge Morath/Magnum Photos; 95. Photo Inge Morath/Magnum Photos; 96. Photo Dennis Stock/Magnum Photos; 100. Photo Inge Morath/Magnum Photos; 101. Courtesy The National Theatre, London. Photo John Haynes; 103. Photo © Bettmann/Corbis; 105. Courtesy Photofest; 108. Photo NBC/The Kobal Collection; 109. Photo courtesy Special Collections Library, University of Michigan. © Al Hirschfeld/Margo Feiden Galleries Ltd., New York. www.alhirschfeld.com; 111. Photo Inge Morath/Magnum Photos; 112. Courtesy the University of Bristol Theatre Collection (ref. BOV/P/000400/11). Photo Derek Balmer; 114. Photo Inge Morath/Magnum Photos; 115. Photo © Corbis Sygma; 119. Photo Inge Morath/Magnum Photos; 120. Photo © Inge Morath/Magnum Photos; 123. Photo courtesy Ronald Grant Archive; 125. Photo Inge Morath/Magnum Photos; 127. Courtesy Photofest; 128. Courtesy The National Theatre, London. Photo Alastair Muir; 131. Photo © Susan Johann; 133. Courtesy Guthrie Theater, Minneapolis. Photo Carol Rosegg; 136. Photo Inge Morath/Magnum Photos; 144. Photo Alfred Eisenstaedt/Getty Images.

# INDEX

Inge Morath and Arthur Miller on the lawn outside their home, Roxbury, Connecticut, 1975